An Englishman's Garden in America

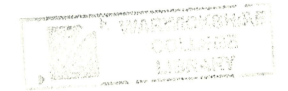

An Englishman's Garden in America

in America

FROM OLD YORK TO NEW YORK

JAMES RAIMES

F

FRANCES LINCOLN LIMITED
PUBLISHERS

Frances Lincoln Limited
4 Torriano Mews, Torriano Avenue
London NW5 2RZ
www.franceslincoln.com

An Englishman's Garden in America
Copyright © James Raimes, 2006

Published in the United States as *Gardening at Ginger* by
Houghton Mifflin Company, 215 Park Avenue South, New York,
New York 10003.

First Frances Lincoln edition 2007

ISBN: 978-0-7112-2797-2

British Library Cataloguing in Publication data
A catalogue record for this book is available from the British Library

Book design by Robert Overholtzer
Map by Leslie Evans
Printed and bound in Singapore

2 4 6 8 9 7 5 3 1

FOR ANN

ACKNOWLEDGMENTS

Thanks to all the friends who read parts of this book and encouraged me: Gillian Darley, Deborah Nevins, Emily McCully, Elizabeth Diggs, Tessa Kale, Sara Cedar Miller, Cynthia Crossen, Ruth Skevington, Leon Back, Joan Arnold, Helen Rogan, Alfred Gingold, and Elizabeth Hess.

Thanks to my family, who read most of the book: Emily, Lucy, Roger and Jenny, Dave Bry, and Matt Szenher; and to Roberta Bernstein and Viki Sand, who are not family and yet are.

Special thanks to the two people at Houghton Mifflin who improved the book in manuscript, Frances Tenenbaum and Luise Erdmann.

And very special thanks to the two people who read every word of this book before it went to Houghton Mifflin: Dorothy James, who commented from the heart; and Ann, great reader and wonderful wife.

CONTENTS

CREATURES

DESIGN

REWARDS

LIFE AFTER DEATH

I Say Daylia, You Say Dahlia

I'M FROM YORK IN ENGLAND and I say *daylia* even though I've lived in New York, where people say *dahlia,* for the last forty years. It's probably because I hardly ever say the word. I forced myself to say *tomaytoes* very soon after arrival in America because I was buying *tomahtoes* regularly and provoking half-concealed laughter at my oh so posh British accent in the local fruit and vegetable store. (Well, excuse me.) And I had no problem saying *skedule,* having seldom had to pronounce *shedule* in England. (If the idea was broached, which was not as often as in America, we tended to favor the word *timetable.*) But those two American pronunciations, *tomaytoes* and *skedule,* are I believe the only ones I have consciously adopted. Dahlias just don't come up in conversation much.

I don't talk about dahlias, even though I am a passionate gardener and I don't grow vegetables. The reason is, I don't grow dahlias either, and no one I know grows them, popular though they obviously are. I can't help being tempted when I see their glorious flowers in catalogues, but in our hardiness zone 5 all dahlias must be treated as annuals, which I don't grow, or lifted and stored carefully every winter, the thought of which worries me. Maybe that's the reason my gardening friends don't grow or talk about them either. At any rate, the only person I do ever talk to about dahlias (and that's not very often) pronounces them the British way because he's my brother Roger, who grows very good-looking specimens at Acaster near York, where we were born and where he still lives.

The American pronunciation, incidentally, could be considered more correct than the British, as the name is derived from the name of the eighteenth-century Swedish botanist, Dr. Anders Dahl (not Dale). But I'm still not going to pronounce it that way. It may be correct but it sounds to my ear *just too too precious, dahling.*

* * * * *

But, hey, pronunciation differences are trivial. In the case of the dahlia, whether we pronounce it the American way or the British way, we all know which plant is being talked about, especially as the plant's botanical name and its common name are the same, which isn't the case with so many other plants. For instance, I have known and loved forget-me-nots since childhood in England, but it was only recently in America, when I started gardening seriously, that I learned their botanical name, *Myosotis.* And the same with Impatience, which must be the easiest annual to grow in North America in sun and shade in city and country alike (well, it does need water, so it's not totally idiot-proof) — anyway, I only recently learned that its botanical name is the same as the common name, only spelled *Impatiens.* I learned at the same time that the plant has at least two other common names, balsam and Busy Lizzie.

Talking of balsam, I remember how surprised I was when I first learned that the wildflower growing just outside the gates at Ginger is *Impatiens balsamina* and so is related not only to the Impatience I had grown in our window box in Brooklyn for years, *Impatiens walleriana,* but also to the potentially invasive *Impatiens glandulifera* that grew alongside the Ouse at Acaster when I was a child. The wildflower at Ginger is ginger-colored, oddly enough, and up to three feet tall, whereas the one I remembered from my childhood is pink and five or six feet tall. But all three of these plants are balsams.

Ginger's wildflower and the British wildflower are also called Touch-me-not, because if you touch their seed pods at the right moment of maturity, they burst open like a jack-in-the-box, spraying seeds all around, in the case of *I. glandulifera* up to 22 feet from the plant. As far as I am concerned, it could have been called "Touch me" because it drew me like a magnet to touch seed pod after seed pod to feel the mini-explosion in my hand. On the other hand, perhaps "Touch-me-not" may be right after all, allowing children the harmless thrill of disobeying the warning. (I would like to see what happens to a bee or butterfly brushing a seed pod inadvertently.)

But the greatest surprise as I read about this plant was that there was no mention of its distinctive smell. The balsam at Ginger doesn't smell, but I can't think of a smell in the world which would be more likely to induce in me a full-blown Proustian "madeleine" moment than the smell of the plant I knew as a child as balsam. I haven't smelled it since I touched the plant as a child, yet it's there in my mind, strong and unlike any other smell I have experienced in all the years since, and if I smelled it anywhere now, even as perfume on a New

York subway passenger, I would instantly be taken back to that hundred yards or so where it grew in the 1940s between the bottom of the Acaster Manor garden and the river. The subway riders around me would be thinking what to say at the next meeting at work or mentally composing a menu for the weekend dinner party or looking forward to seeing their children again that evening. I would be smelling and touching balsam and walking along with the Ouse on my left, past the dam and the locks and the salmon passage, then further to the South Ings on my right, colorful with wildflowers in the summer, often flooded in the winter (and now a Site of Special Scientific Interest) and back past an underground pump known mysteriously as a ram (a technical term, I later learned, short for reciprocating ram) which pumped water from the river to the Manor grounds. It's no longer in use, but my walk wouldn't be complete without the mysterious regular slow beating-heart thump, thump, thump deep below where I would be kneeling listening. By the time my subway stop came into view, my head would be full of the thumping and full of the loud warbling cries of the curlews circling high and wide overhead. Who was with me? Will I ever smell that balsam again?

* * * * *

When Ann revisits London and I revisit York, we are each going home (or coming home, depending on viewpoint). We notice the differences since we lived there, we see what has remained the same, then we go home, or come home, again to New York. For a British-born American gardener, at home in both countries, visits inevitably invite comparisons. What are the differences, beyond the trivial differences of pronunciation, the differences in common names, the differences in the color of a plant's flowers?

The big differences are in history, wideness of practice, and climate. The British already had a gardening history, with several changes of fashion, by the time Jefferson was gardening at Monticello, and their history has deepened and broadened as it has lengthened. Drive around Britain, and you see good gardening at every level of society. Old city parks are beautiful, old visitable country estates are breathtaking. But so are many small gardens in country villages, and so are many small gardens in the suburbs. The heir to the throne gardens well enough to earn some paragraphs in future histories, but look at the allotments around the country to see how lovingly soil can be worked by city dwellers for food or flowers. Europe is the old country to Americans, and to American eyes, mine included, it seems that the British — so many of them in such a small area — have all gardened for ever.

It's not true, of course, but gardening in Britain is impressive enough to seem exaggeratedly enviable to American eyes. Our last visit to Yorkshire took us to Newby Hall which, even in late spring when most of its perennials had barely surfaced above the soil, struck me as the most beautiful garden I had ever seen on any continent. (I have been gardening for only ten years and visiting gardens for only six or seven, but I would be surprised if many more years would change my mind.) I can't help envying British gardeners. But what is it I envy?

Well, specifically, it's their climate. The climate is the difference that makes all the difference. The climate is at the bottom of the list of things most American tourists would say they like about Britain, but it's the envy of all gardeners. American gardeners must cope with either far colder winters or far hotter and drier summers, or both, than their British counterparts. My gardening year in New York is shorter by several months than Roger's in York.

But I come back to New York knowing that the nine acre site I garden in Columbia County is as beautiful in its own way as many a similar site in North Yorkshire, and excited that there will always be ways to improve it. And after I have chased away the green-eyed monster yet again, I relax in the knowledge of what gardeners share in all countries: not just tools and skills and a botanical language but, in the best practitioners, a set of values and a passion that are recognizable, however different their aesthetics, and however tied to a particular site each gardener ineluctably is.

INTRODUCTIONS

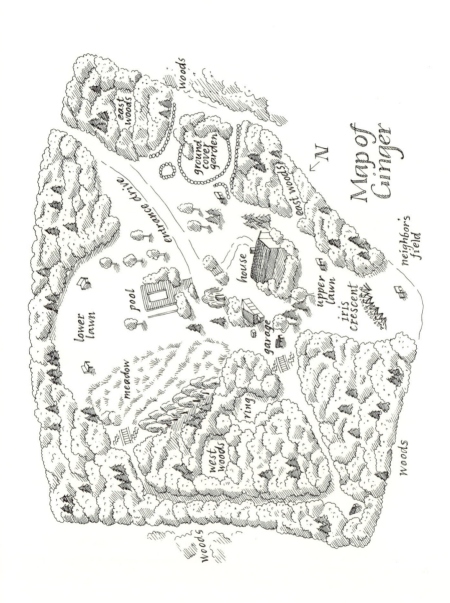

Map of Ginger

N

woods

east woods

ground cover garden

east woods?

entrance drive

house

upper lawn

neighbor's field

pool

iris crescent

lower lawn

garage

meadow

ring

west woods

woods

woods

CHAPTER 1

Ginger

THE PLACE HAS A STREET ADDRESS, a name, and a nickname. Ann and I learned the street address when we called the owners, who had placed the ad for it in the *New York Times*. We learned its name only after we had bought the place, and the nickname came later.

We had for a long time owned a cabin called Fred near Catskill, in Greene County, New York, and we had decided we should graduate at last to a *house* house, one that we could live in year-round instead of just visiting on weekends in the warm months, and one where I could garden, something I had been wanting to do for a long time.

We had bought Fred in 1971. It was spacious, with two floors, but thrown together some years before for no money and in disrepair from not having been used for five years. It was full of dust and critters, and it was leaking. When we first saw it, we thought we had driven a long way for nothing, but when we walked around to the back, we stopped in our tracks and said "Wow." The people who built the place must have said the same thing when they first saw this spectacular view. Both floors had huge windows looking out to a big stretch of the Catskill Mountains. They were four miles or more away, but looked close enough to reach out and stroke their hairy slopes.

Why the name Fred? While we were negotiating with the seller, we invited an architect friend to look at it with us. He walked around it, tapped the walls, jumped up and down on the floors, shook his head, and finally climbed through a hole in the floor to a crawl space underneath to see what he suspected: its joists were too far apart and spanned too great a distance, and the whole place was badly anchored to the sloping ground. He pronounced a quick and final judgment: it was a dog. In England, where Ann and I had grown up, we had never heard that term applied to things, but we got the message. The place was worthless; no way should we buy it. But we loved its wooded acreage, its casual character, and that spectacular view. And the price was ridiculously low. We bought it, and we proceeded to have three decades of great times there on weekends and during summer vacations. It had electricity and running water, but no phone, no TV, no radio, and no address.

But the place we loved needed a name. At that time we were in the habit, for some reason, of calling all dogs, and especially dogs that chased our car, Fred. Well, if all dogs were Fred, and our cabin was a dog, then our cabin must be Fred. It was of course a nickname, which in the spirit of the early seventies we treated as a name. To the straightest people and officials, we referred to "our cabin," but to our daughters, Emily and Lucy, and to all our friends and all of their friends it was always Fred. Lucy owns it now, and it's still Fred.

So now (that is, seven years ago and nearly thirty years after we bought Fred), real estate agents were leading us around houses in much better condition than Fred. We were in Columbia County, which our close friends Roberta and Viki in Kinderhook loved, but so far we had been disappointed in what we had seen. Then I remembered I had in my wallet a tiny *New York Times* ad that described a place within minutes of Chatham, which we knew was near Roberta and Viki, and also within minutes of the Taconic Parkway. It was more expensive than the houses we had been seeing, but the ad also mentioned "perennial gardens," which was the reason I had kept the ad. I felt that we couldn't not at least see the place, so we called the owners, got the street address, and agreed on a time later that day to look at it. Ann and I promised each other that we wouldn't even consider buying anything that expensive unless we said "Wow!" at first sight, as we had at Fred.

"Street address" is something of a misnomer, because in the two minutes it takes to drive there from the Taconic, the roads become rapidly smaller and more treed, until finally you are on a wooded dead-end dirt road, and the property is the last house on the left at the end. When we drove up the driveway, we felt we had entered a secluded domain deep in the country.

We parked at the end of the driveway under an enormous weeping willow. There was a swimming pool to our right, a garage straight ahead, and a ranch-style house up a little to our left. Thin strips of garden surrounded the end of the driveway, the pool, and the house. The gardens were small and the house was modest, but as soon as we got out of the car we felt good.

We walked up one of the two sets of steps to a large wooden front deck and entered the house through a front door with glass in it. The owners took us from an entrance hall to a spacious living room with a large picture window on one side and on the other, a French door with many windows on either side of it, opening onto the same front deck we had come in from. The living room flowed into a dining room, with a sliding glass door leading to a back deck, and it also flowed into a kitchen with a door with glass in it, also leading to the back deck. There were no doors between these four central rooms, only doors to the outdoors. The doors that did exist indoors gave privacy to the bedrooms and bathrooms on either side of these central rooms, but the master bedroom had a sliding glass door onto the back deck and many windows, and its bathroom had large windows and a huge mirror up against one of them, so we looked at an outdoors doubled in its reflection. Ann had been yearning for a house with a lot of light, and here was a house whose many big windows and glass doors made it lighter than almost any conventional house we had walked through in our lives. Ann writes textbooks, one of which has been very successful and several of which need constant revision. She could see one of the guest bedrooms doubling as her office. When she looked up every so often from her computer, she would look out onto lawn, trees, and birds.

The gardens were very pleasant, but to me they were exciting — as probably any well-cared-for gardens with plenty of different plants in them would have been to someone itching to get his hands dirty in soil. But what attracted us most about the place was its siting. The buildings and gardens were in the middle of four acres of sloping lawn. Woods surrounding the lawn gave a sense of enclosure, but within that enclosure the place was open. From the entrance hall and living room at the front, we couldn't help looking through the large windows downward (which was to the north) across a calming seventy-five-yard expanse of green. There was a similar seventy-five-yard view up a slope (to the south) from the dining room, kitchen, and master bedroom, and yet another to the west from windows on that side of the living room, master bedroom, and bathroom. The lower lawn expanded at the bottom to a width of a hundred and fifty yards, and the upper lawn contracted at the top to about twenty-five yards. The setting was parklike — on a small scale, but definitely parklike. When we got back in the car under the weeping willow, turned on the engine, and started driving out of earshot of the owners, we glanced at each other, raised our eyebrows, nodded, and said a quiet "Wow!" to each other.

We learned the name of the place some hours after we had bought it. We were walking around the empty, echoing house with the sellers after the closing when we casually asked them whether the place had ever been called anything. They were quite surprised that we didn't know. We had inspected the house and the grounds in minute detail, but somehow we hadn't noticed the sign on a wooden post at the entrance: Willow Hill. "Oh, okay," we said, and looked at each other. "Hmm." Later, when the sellers had left, we realized we had both had the same thought: much as we loved the place, we weren't crazy about its name.

It was certainly appropriate for the place, which is on a slope, with a line of fourteen big, beautiful weeping willows at the west side of the lower lawn, and that magnificent weeping willow in the very center of the property, where you park your car. But there was something — we weren't quite sure what — wrong with the name. Maybe it gave an impression of grandeur, which the place didn't have, or maybe it sounded too suburban for a secluded place at the end of a dead-end dirt road in the country. Or maybe we felt that if the place had to have a name (which it didn't, as the street address was perfectly adequate to identify it), we didn't want someone else's name, we wanted to name it ourselves. Isn't giving a name to something one of the great joys and responsibilities of ownership? Children's names, so intimate and at the same time so public, are one of the most important decisions parents make in their lives. Naming pets clinches the bond between owners and their dogs or cats or tortoises. A home, for us, was in the same category, and we would never have named this place Willow Hill.

But what would we have named it? Should we change it? If so, what to? We had no ideas. The previous owners had left us some bathroom towels with the name Willow Hill embroidered on them, like the name of a bed-and-breakfast. Their color suited the guest bathroom. Should we keep them there, hanging over the bars so that the name was displayed? Or use them for more mundane, domestic clean-up jobs until they wore out?

Then, some months later, when the name of the place was still a subliminal irritant, a woman knocked on our door and told us that she had grown up on the property thirty years earlier and wanted to revisit her childhood haunts. Could she look around? We spent a pleasant hour, hearing how much the place had meant to her, seeing her venture into her old bedroom, which hadn't changed at all, and into the kitchen, which had changed completely, and learning all sorts of things about the place. We asked whether her family had had a name for the place. "Oh, sure," she said, "and it made me feel really good to see it still there on the wooden post at the entrance. My dad thought of the name and put the sign there. I'm so glad you have kept it." So now it seemed we had some obligation to keep the name. Well, it was relatively harmless.

When we mentioned the name to Emily and Lucy (great names for great people, though we say it ourselves), their reactions were, successively, politely negative and openly scornful. Lucy started calling it Willy Hill, which I liked a lot, but it wasn't long before she came up with an even better name. Ann loves the Fred Astaire and Ginger Rogers movies, and a close friend had given us for our twentieth wedding anniversary a poster of twelve stills from that classic, romantic "Cheek to Cheek" dance sequence in *Top Hat* in which Ginger Rogers wears the feathery white dress that Ann considers the best dress ever worn by a woman in the history of the world. Lucy had herself given Ann a birthday present of what looked like a photograph of Ann dancing with Fred Astaire. She had digitally grafted Ann's head onto Ginger Rogers's body. Obviously the new house should be called Ginger.

That sounded good. It must be that our family just doesn't like traditional names for houses. We wouldn't have dreamed of calling our cabin Mountain View. Willow Hill remains its official name, but we have never made it a part of our mailing address, and when I give directions to people visiting for the first time, I tell them there's a street number on a metal 911 sign at the entrance and don't mention the sign with the name on it. Ann has been somewhat slower than the rest of us to adopt the nickname as a name, but she's halfway there. She calls it W.H., indicating that she can't quite get her mouth around the official name. Neither of us would want to throw out the bath towels with the old name on them. And I notice that I haven't removed the sign at the entrance.

But there's another reason for my playing down the original name. (Confession hour.) Since I have been gardening passionately in this place for the last seven years, I have become aware that there are several outstanding gardens with the word "Hill" in their names. North Hill, for instance, about which its owners Joe Eck and Wayne Winterowd wrote a book that I keep picking up to learn or relearn something about gardening, knowing that I'm going to enjoy their prose, their photographs, and their passion every time I do so. And Wave Hill in the Bronx, a destination for over a hundred thousand garden lovers a year. Compared to places like that, ours will for many years be way down in the minor leagues. It's a very good looking place, and we love it, but if ever I were to call our place Willow Hill when talking to other serious gardeners, I don't think I could keep those ironic quotation marks out of my voice. But then I probably wouldn't call it Ginger when talking to them either, let alone Willy Hill.

CHAPTER 2

Digging into the Past

WHEN WE BOUGHT GINGER seven years ago, back in the days when it went by the name of Willow Hill, I wasn't a gardener, but I was definitely an armchair gardener. I owned two books of gardening essays, Katharine White's *Onward and Upward in the Garden* and Eleanor Perenyi's *Green Thoughts;* and I owned two gardening reference books: the Reader's Digest *Illustrated Guide to Gardening* and William Robinson's *The English Flower Garden,* an 1883 book given to us by our friend Debbie "Gardener to the Stars" Nevins, who had written the introduction to its 1984 reissue. This hundred-year-old book, we learned, had a very special place in the history of British gardening, but Debbie herself was more of an inspiration to an aspiring gardener than the classic she was reintroducing. We call her "Gardener to the Stars" because she has designed gardens for the most famous newspaper owner in the world, the most famous movie studio head in the world, a Number 1 tennis player in the world, the creator of the most famous coffee brand in the world, one of the most famous clothing designers in the country, one of New York's most

famous caterers, and one of New York's most famous
financiers. Those are just a few of her many clients.
Debbie is not a large woman, but she has an intimidat-
ingly large reputation in the world I was about to venture into.

So, back down to earth again. When we bought Ginger, I had no experience to speak of, and I had no tools.
What I had was desire and enthusiasm, and I started
calling myself a gardener immediately. Ann gave me a
ladder for my birthday, and Emily and Lucy gave me a
bulb planter, a watering can, and Frances Tenenbaum's
Encyclopedia of Garden Plants. I bought a spade and fork
and trowel and gloves and rake and wheelbarrow and
chain saw and loppers, and I bought pruning shears,
which in England, I remembered, we had called seca-
teurs. I added to my five-book gardening library by buying Hugh Johnson's *Principles of Gardening,* subscribed
to *Horticulture* and *The American Gardener,* and ordered
White Flower Farm's and Wayside Garden's catalogues.
Roberta and Viki introduced us to Ruth and Leon, who
garden magnificently three minutes from Ginger and
are very generous with their knowledge and with plants.
I tried to keep the perennial beds tidy, and within a couple of years I had started clearing the woods in the west
part of the property and moving plants I could see were
crowding one another.

Friends and acquaintances asked whether my English background accounted for the passion with which I
had thrown myself into my new activity. They still ask
me about it seven years later. I think they assume that,
having spent most of my first three decades in a country which is the envy of the garden world — well, how
could I not want to put my knowledge and skills to work
in a garden, now that I owned one? The British all have

green thumbs, don't they? Ruth is an ex-Brit, like us, and she certainly has one.

My first thoughts were: I wasn't a gardener when I was in England, so I couldn't have gained gardening knowledge or skills there. I didn't know about plants or garden design or the history of gardens, and I didn't think of learning about them. I didn't own or read any gardening books, never read a gardening magazine, and never visited a garden on my own. It had been here in America in the last thirty years that my desire to garden, fed by countless lunches in New York City's Central Park and regular visits to Brooklyn's Prospect Park, had steadily grown until I was able to satisfy it at last by buying Ginger. People who knew me in England would never have predicted that later in my life in America I would be out there in the perennial beds or in the woods as many months in the year as the climate would allow, or that if the weather or my health kept me from digging and pruning and weeding, I would be reading or thinking about those activities. I would never have predicted it myself. There were plenty of subjects I threw myself passionately into in England back then, but gardening wasn't one of them.

But then I got to wondering. Gardens and the beautiful English countryside were certainly a large part of my privileged middle-class childhood and youth, almost as large a part as the buildings I lived in. And when I thought more about it, I realized that if there were two places in the world that had over the years symbolized for me manmade and wild natural beauty, two places that I had been carrying with me not only in treasured memory but very close to the center of my emotional self, they were the garden at Acaster Malbis, near York, where my sister, Faith, my brother, Roger, and I were

born, and the moors at Hutton-le-Hole, forty miles
north of York, where we moved after our parents died.
The first represents forever the lost happiness of my
childhood, the second all the outsize desires, frustrated
and fulfilled, of adolescence and young adulthood. And
yes, all these years later I could see that they had indeed been present, even if partially buried and barely
acknowledged, among the images I had brought with
me from old York to New York. They had surfaced in my
motivations as a gardener and in my thoughts about
gardening.

Faith was eleven, Roger was nine, and I was five when
our mother died of lung cancer. Two years later, when I
was seven, our father died of a heart attack, and we were
orphans. Our guardian, an uncle, arranged for us to
move from Acaster Manor (almost as grand a place as
its name implies) to a much smaller country cottage in
Hutton-le-Hole, a village as quaint as its name at the
edge of the North Yorkshire moors. (Talking of names,
Ann, a Londoner accustomed to addresses with street
numbers, couldn't believe it when she met me that my
address was Hammer and Hand House, Hutton-le-Hole,
York.) My uncle and his second wife, whom we called
Aunt P, had a cottage (Ashtrees) in Hutton, and Aunt
P's sister, whom we called Aunt B, lived with us and
looked after us in another cottage (abbreviated to Hammer) on the opposite side of the village. They were both
fine gardeners.

I felt good in their gardens in a way that I haven't felt
in many, perhaps most, American gardens, and not just
because our family owned the Hutton gardens. My
aunts' gardens offered that wonderful sense of calm that
comes from the carefully proportioned arrangement of
established trees, closely mowed lawn, crisp edges,

flowering plants, and solid green hedges framing and enclosing everything. In the case of Aunt P's garden, which was relatively long and thin, there was also great interest in the variety of experiences it offered as you walked its length.

I find it difficult, however, to describe in detail what it was that felt good in them. Partly this is because of the amount of time that has elapsed since I walked in them, and partly because I took them for granted at the time and didn't pay the sort of attention to them that I had to pay to academics and sport, for instance, or that I wanted to pay to friends or to the arts, or, more relevant in this context, to the moors. It felt good to stroll in these back gardens on a hot summer afternoon before sitting down to tea and scones and cake on the lawn, but their sense of enclosure, precious to me now in memory, was not what an energetic boy wanted back then, particularly when a huge expanse of beautiful wild countryside beckoned within easy walking distance.

Hutton-le-Hole is picturesque in itself and in its setting. Nestled in a depression at the edge of the moors, it is nevertheless very open and airy. Three roads dip down into it and meet to become two, one on each side of a small stream. Its most prominent feature is its village green, wide and long, cropped close by geese and black-faced sheep, spreading around and between the groups of stone houses with red-tiled roofs, on either side of the stream, and on either side of the two roads. The village is mentioned in the guidebooks, and you can see pictures of it on the Web. You can see white wooden railings lining roads and paths over the many gentle slopes and on either side of the bridges over the stream. Tour buses descended in such numbers at weekends that a large parking lot had to be built at the edge of the village to protect its vistas and the grass of its green.

Above the village the moors stretch over 550 square miles west to the Vale of York, and north and east to the sea. Its dales are green or brown with trees, bracken, and small fields bounded by stone walls or hedges, but on much of its gently rolling expanse all you see is heather, which is gray-green or brown much of the year but in the fall is bright pink and purple all the way to the horizon in every direction.

This wild landscape with enormous skies was a magnet for an adolescent in a way that a garden manicured by an aunt couldn't hope to be. I remember it in the way that the speaker in Dylan Thomas's "Fern Hill" remembers the country of his green and golden carefree youth. I chased Emperor moths for miles over the clumps of heather with my butterfly net. Skylarks kept up a continuous high warbling and trilling overhead, and grouse exploded upward as I came near their nests on the ground, with a sort of quacking, "Go back, go back, go back!" Curlews wouldn't let me come near: they flew high when I was still a distance away, and their loud, upward-sweeping cries, warbling faster and faster and higher and higher up the scale and ending in a long high trill, stood my hair on end.

Compared to this open wildness, my aunts' gardens were tame and confining, but now that I am gardening, I have to give them the credit they deserve. Our own back garden, where Aunt B spent much of her time, was a small and gracious haven, with two old twisted Bramley apple trees at the end of a lawn, a sunny border of annuals and perennials on the left, and a shady border on the right. Its central lawn, divided by a curving path of flagstones into two rectangles, was the turf of blackbirds and robins, the latter smaller than their American counterparts, hopping, listening, then tugging worms from the ground. English daisies, also diminutive compared to American daisies, were the lawn's prettiest weeds. Daffodils flowered in the spring under the apples.

I liked sitting in a deck chair in that garden, reading, with the liquid songs of thrushes in the apple trees and the hum of bees among the flowers. But what flowers? What did Aunt B grow in the borders on the right and left and in the border at the far end of the garden? I remember temperamental clematis on the fence to the left; I remember nasturtiums, whose leaves we ate; I remember honesty, whose seed pods Aunt B would include in dried flower arrangements; and I remember the rose 'Peace', which produced one perfect bloom after another. I remember red-hot pokers one year, delphiniums another year. And I remember some names of flowers which I have never heard pronounced since Aunt B pronounced them — for instance, eschscholzia ("es-kol-cha") and aubrietia ("au-bree-sha"), the latter spelled differently in many American reference works (aubrieta) and presumably pronounced differently — but I don't know whether Aunt B grew them. Which leads me to note for my own gardening purposes at Ginger that it is overall proportion and structure that stay in the mind, not individual flowering plants, however much they attract us.

Aunt P's garden was considerably bigger and had been a garden for a longer time than Aunt B's. One section led invitingly into another and was called by one knowledgeable friend "worthy of Gertrude Jekyll." The ground floor of the back of the house had been built into a slope, and Aunt P had had that bank of earth dug out so you could walk out from the house onto a paved patio. On the back wall of the house she grew an es-paliered pear tree, and placed at its feet many stone troughs, which she filled with alpine plants. On the other side of the patio, opposite the back wall of the house, she had stones banked to support the next section of the garden several feet above. Aunt P filled every niche among these stones with small mounding perennials, creating a multitextured rock garden around a bench and chairs on the patio. Stone steps with a wooden railing led up to the next section of the garden above.

From the top of the stone steps you walked onto a lawn with a fine old Bramley apple tree and daffodils under it. Perennial borders surrounded the lawn on three sides: the one on the left had a trellis hung with clematis and roses, the one ahead of you a post hung with a different clematis and a different rose, the one on the right filled with shrubs and fruit trees.

The next section of the garden, concealed by the central border with the post, consisted of rows of vegetables. Then a small gate led into a shaded section, surrounded by damson plum trees, a barn, and an open-fronted one-story stone shed. Aunt P had planted ferns and shade-loving perennials in this area and placed chairs and a bench in the small shed.

From this shaded section of the garden, you walked ahead through a wide gate across a public path and through another wide gate into a field, one of many fields climbing in parallel strips up a moderately steep slope to a wood at the top, where the property ended. The bottom left corner of Aunt P's field was made into a "fruit cage," a fenced-in area where my uncle grew blackberries, raspberries, strawberries, gooseberries, red-currants, and blackcurrants. (When I wrote the word "blackcurrants," my mouth watered at the thought of fruit not tasted for over thirty years. Many Americans have never tasted them. And — another aside — I gave Ann her engagement ring in this fruit cage.)

So if you walked up to the top of the field, you would have experienced in turn the intimacy of a rock garden patio, the openness and color of a lawn surrounded by perennials, a hidden vegetable garden, a restful area in the shade of fruit trees, and then the long open slope of this field. Turning round at the top you would look back down over the garden, over the rooftops of the village, ahead to a wooded hill behind the village, and, to the left of the hill, the moors stretching away into the distance.

What a nice garden. In fact, both gardens — our own small one at Hammer, which Aunt B gardened, and Aunt P's at Ashtrees — were much admired by visitors. When I came back from America to visit them in later years, I enjoyed them with a combination of poignant memories and more objective critical pleasure, but when I lived in Hutton there was another reason for my inability to appreciate them fully. It was simply that my aunts were not my mother and could never be, and the charm of their gardens could never compare to that of the Acaster garden, the paradise I had lost.

Acaster Manor's five-and-a-half-acre garden had been designed toward the end of the nineteenth century. In 1897 a curved line of copper beeches was planted on the right side of the property as you looked from the house. By the middle of the twentieth century, when I knew them, they were massive, and they are still there in the twenty-first century. Immediately in front of the house was a large lawn, and past the lawn a manmade lake with an island in the middle of it, large enough to be an attractive garden in itself at one time, with roses, clematis, and lupines. During World War II, I vaguely remember geese were kept on it. Foxes couldn't reach them there.

In the middle of the lawn between the house and the lake were a number of formal features, symmetrically located on a central axis. They were at their best in the early decades of the twentieth century, as was the whole garden, when three or four gardeners cared for it. There had been a big holly tree in the middle of this area, and in the middle of the holly a room, complete with door. That would have been a perfect play-place for kids, but it had gone before we were born. What remained of these features were still of real fascination to a child in the 1940s: a low rock garden, a fountain, and a circular area enclosed by clipped box hedges. All of these are gone now, leaving a fine, unobstructed view from the house over the large lawn, down to the lake. There used to be two yews, huge in the mid-twentieth century, on either side of the lawn. At the base of one, which is still alive, a semicircle of carved masonry enclosed a natural play area, complete with a collection of small stones and shells. That was my play-place.

If I wanted adventure, I could punt on the lake around the island or walk into the woods to the right of the lake and beyond it. At one point the walk consisted of stepping-stones across a boggy area fed by water from a small pond, which we didn't explore when we were children because it was hidden by rampant bamboo, but it was revealed in the 1980s. The stepping-stones led to a path which divided: in one direction I continued around the lake, in the other I entered the woods, where I soon came across a "folly," a stone arch taken from the ruins of Saint Andrews Church, in nearby Bishopthorpe.

If I continued from the stepping-stones on the path

anti-clockwise around the lake, I passed statuary, a sun-
dial, a perennial border, and a line of Lombardy poplars.
Returning home on the train from trips to Scarborough,
I looked out of the window when I knew we were approaching Acaster and got excited when I saw those
poplars gradually coming into view in the distance.

Acaster would remain "home" long after we had to
leave it and long after our guardians had to sell it for us,
but it was the garden, not the large house, to which I
would have returned if I could. I wish I had known it in
its prime. Aunt B's and Aunt P's gardens I did know in
their prime, and in their cases I wish I had been able to
appreciate them better at the time. As it was, a newly
homeless preteenager seems in memory to have ex-
hausted Aunt B's garden in minutes and Aunt P's in a
quarter of an hour, whereas as a child I hadn't been able
to exhaust Acaster's garden in days, day after day, summer after summer.

Revisiting England in later years, I was able to talk as
an adult with my aunts about their passion and skills at
Hutton-le-Hole, and with Roger, who has been living in
a different house at Acaster right next to the manor,
about our old family garden. Now as a gardener I think
that it may have been the memory of these three gardens that made me decide that gardens were places I
liked to be in, and, further, that a garden was something
that I wanted to create and care for. No, I didn't have
a British green thumb when I started gardening here,
but I did have rich memories of British gardens in the
formative years of my life. Certainly, if I could design as
well as my nineteenth-century ancestor and garden as
well as my aunts, there could be a chance that someone
would remember Ginger's garden later in the twenty-
first century.

ACTIVITY

CHAPTER 3

Moving Plants

A FEW WEEKS BEFORE we bought Ginger, I walked around the perennial beds and the shrubs and trees in the lawn with one of the owners. The individual beds were not large, but there were ten of them, and the owners had clearly liked buying plants. As we walked and talked, I found that I knew many of the plants from having lived a long time in the world and been curious, but there were also many that I didn't know. I got the owner to repeat their names, wrote them down, and hoped that I was managing to spell them right and that I could remember how to pronounce them. I checked them out later in my encyclopedia and found that *Cornus* was dogwood, that *Kolkwitzia* was beautybush, and *Taxus* was yew. *Weigela* didn't have a common name. Meanwhile, it was early winter, so nothing was in flower and not much was in leaf. I looked forward to seeing all these plants in the spring or summer or whenever they put on a show.

I asked who mowed the lawn and which local nursery they favored. The answer in each case was Callander's, and Callander's also "opened" the place every spring

25

and "cleaned it up" at the end of the fall, terms which conjured up a picture I wasn't entirely happy with: that of professionals preparing the place for clueless owners to have their fun with in the summer and fall, then cleaning up after them in such a way that they couldn't do too much harm in the winter. However, I renewed the contract with Callander's and haven't yet weaned myself from my reliance on them for these particular jobs. All other jobs, except the biggest, I took on myself. Gardening for me was, still is, and always will be learning by doing.

During our first days of ownership, Ann and I started doing the essentials: buying beds, tables, chairs, kitchenware, and all the other things needed to furnish an empty house. The outside could wait. I couldn't do much out there, as it was winter, and anyway, the outside was already furnished, wasn't it?

Come to think of it, I can only remember one instance of a seller's taking plants as well as furniture from a property. When the owner of the Crown Inn next door to us at Hutton-le-Hole sold the pub, he horrified Aunt B by cutting off all the roses covering its front wall at about knee height, taking the roots and the bottom two feet of the plants, and leaving the dead canes splayed against the wall. Perhaps he had itemized the roses as his possessions in the contract of sale. No, he wasn't that sort of person. And anyway, I wonder how often plants figure in contracts. In our case, of course, the sellers couldn't have carted off truckloads of plants after having included "perennial gardens" in the description of what they were selling. We know of apartment and house sellers who unscrew light bulbs and towel racks and strip their places clean of everything worth a few cents or a dollar — it's more common in

Europe than in America — but stripping a garden down to the soil, no.

Anyway, those open views across lawn, with the sparse furnishing of a shrub or a few small trees here and there, were precisely what we liked about the place, and I wasn't about to start filling them up. Whether I was inside looking out or outside walking around, my eyes liked wandering over and resting on the gentle green curves of lawn or, after an overnight snow, on the amazing sudden white. Inside and outside we subscribed to a simple aesthetic: if the structure is pleasing, keep what you put into it simple and spare. Don't get tempted to clutter it with stuff.

I didn't do much to change the gardens for a year. On the advice of our Callander's contact, Heather Field (how about that for a perfect name for someone with her job?), I watched to see what plants were growing where and how they behaved over the warm months before deciding whether I wanted to rearrange anything. I walked around with a notebook, surprised and delighted most of the time, and compiled lists of jobs I could see facing me. I made an entrance into the west woods, and once inside, I made paths and cleared out weedy shrubs. When it was dark or wet, I read books of essays about gardening and a few fine general books on the subject, and started trying to match the varieties of peony and daylily in our perennial beds with the color pictures in the plant encyclopedia. "There are several good varieties of peony, and several good varieties of daylily," the previous owner had said, without telling me their variety names. Maybe she didn't remember them. I still haven't identified them all.

But as soon as that first year was over, I started rearranging things, and found that it took a very great deal of my time. A neighbor had told me that she learned everything she knew about gardening from an English woman who spent most of her time moving plants from place to place. I had thought that this was a rather odd thing to learn and that she and her friend were perhaps eccentric. Surely, to be continually *moving* plants, whose distinguishing characteristic as a life form is to remain in one spot throughout life, is to confess that you have continually been doing something wrong. Aunt P and Aunt B were superb gardeners, and I didn't remember their moving a single plant.

However, it wasn't long before I began to suspect that my memory of how my aunts gardened was deficient. Or if my memory was accurate, I began to suspect that my aunts had already moved plenty of plants to establish the gardens I remembered. At any rate, I changed my views on the subject during the course of our second year at Ginger, so much so that if someone asked Ann what on earth I was doing out there all day long, she would most likely answer, "Oh, he's probably moving plants from place to place."

I may at the time have been doing any number of other things: watering, weeding, pruning, composting, mulching, or lopping, for instance, all to preserve and polish the status quo, but it was also true that I was now spending more of my time changing the status quo. I was beginning to make the garden ours. I was moving plants continually. Since then I have never stopped moving plants, and I never will stop moving plants. I now think it is an absolutely essential component of gardening, confirmed by one friend who said that the best gardener she knows doesn't feel she has really owned a plant until she has moved it three times. Ruth and Leon are forever moving plants. I can't now understand how a gardener would *not* move plants the whole time.

If you look at a photograph of a plant or a whole garden, you are looking at one artificial moment in time, but the plant and all the plants in a garden live in real time, which is continuous time. And living, for a plant, means growing to maturity. And most plants in a garden are not yet mature. In real time, plants grow sideways as well as upward before and after the finger touches the camera button. Time changes a garden from seeming empty one year to being just right two years later to being crowded two years after that. The previous owners had bought a lot of fine trees, shrubs, and perennials, which were on the whole growing well, but one of the reasons I spent so much time moving them around in our second and subsequent years of ownership was to give them more space in which to grow even better.

Seeds grow into plants, acorns grow into oaks — we all know that. But we tend to forget it when we are in a hurry to fill in spaces in our gardens. Here is a list of the shrubs and young trees clustered within twenty feet of the front of the house when we bought it: two red maples directly in front, a kousa dogwood, a Callery pear, a star magnolia, a white pine, and a Japanese maple to the right as you looked down to the lower lawn; and to the left as you looked down, a Harry Lauder Walking Stick, a 'Snowdrift' crab apple, a river birch, a Russian olive, and a weeping white birch. Doesn't just listing all those trees say "too much"? Oh, and there were five 'PeeGee' hydrangeas in a line also directly in front, behind the red maples. The trees and shrubs, fine specimens individually, would have grown into one another, competing not only aesthetically for attention and appreciation but biologically for sunlight, water, nutrients, and survival. Furthermore, if all throve and you couldn't see the house from the rest of the property, which may conceivably have been what the previous owners wanted, from inside the house you couldn't see the rest of the property, which was the opposite of what we wanted.

So for us it was like living with the previous owners' furnishings, furnishings that were growing and would keep growing, in this case to become thicker and thicker outside curtains. The openness that was so attractive to us, the long views from our windows, would be gone in a few years, when moving the plants to reclaim the views would be difficult and expensive. We had to deal with their future now.

Very wealthy people, such as Debbie Nevins's clients, can impose their vision (or her vision) of a future garden on their land within weeks or months. They have earth moved, lakes and ha-has dug, walls and steps built, mature trees planted, sod laid down, thousands of plants and bulbs dug in, and there they have it: a new garden. Even if we had wanted to clear out all the previous owners' plant furnishings and install our own, we couldn't have afforded it, and it would have been a truly awful confession of bad judgment in buying the place. No, we liked the site and we liked the plants they had bought, but we knew we would regret leaving some of them where they were.

So we moved some of the trees directly in front and to the right, and we moved the five hydrangeas. "We" in this case means that Ann and I decided which plants to move and where to put them, with Heather's helpful advice and Callander's providing the labor. After this first important job, I have done all the moving of plants myself. Ann and I decide on anything that would affect the immediate neighborhood of the house. At the outer limits of the property in any direction, I seldom consult her, and so far there have been few problems.

In the ideal garden, three requirements should be satisfied whenever a plant is moved:

1. The plant should grow just as well, and look just as good, if not better, in its new position.
2. The place the plant is taken from should look just as good, or better, for its removal.
3. The place the plant is moved to should look just as good, or better, for its introduction there.

If those requirements are met, it should follow that after each plant is moved, the ideal overall garden will perform better and look better. Our garden, like most gardens, is not ideal, but on the whole I am satisfied with our first transplantings. The Russsian olive was badly mauled by deer in its new position in the upper lawn and died within a year, but the red maples are thriving, one in the middle of the lower lawn and the other at the bottom of the lower lawn. The white pine has survived its move up to the southwest corner of the upper lawn, and although the star magnolia was also mauled by deer or raccoons in its new position on the eastern edge of the upper lawn, it will grow up fine, I think. The trees now have much more space for growing sideways, and they will be appreciated as specimens better. And the views from the house are much better.

I have myself spent countless hours moving plants smaller than trees: shrubs, from two to ten feet tall, and perennials, from two inches to three feet tall. In each case, an aesthetic decision was involved, and then the work: making sure that the conditions of the soil in the new position were right for the plant and that the light, water, and nutrients available there were sufficient for its future growth (sites can vary enormously, even within a quarter of an acre); then digging up the plant, making sure that enough of its roots were retained to support future growth, keeping the roots moist, digging a big hole in the new position, moistening it, improving the soil with compost, placing the plant in the hole at exactly the right depth, firming the soil, watering it again thoroughly, and mulching around it. How many plants have I done all this for? A lot of them are small, but I'm definitely talking thousands.

The shrubs I have moved include a dozen ten-foot lilacs, several four-foot barberries, several four-foot winged euonymuses, and two ten-foot Roses of Sharon. Ann wasn't keen for me to move the Roses of Sharon, as they were growing extremely well where they were and they bloomed profusely when there was not much else in bloom. They had been planted by the previous owners to constitute a sort of screen or sheltering hedge on one side of a hot tub they planned to install on a concrete square outside their bedroom. They had given up on the hot tub, leaving us with an unsightly square of concrete outside the bedroom that was now ours and those Roses of Sharon. We had the concrete removed. I thought the double magenta blossoms of the Roses of Sharon ugly, even more so when they were covered with Japanese beetles, and especially because they were close to the house, acting as a screen to block off the view of a magnificent willow behind them and an attractive entrance to the west woods farther behind the willow. For three years I moaned as these plants grew bigger and bigger until Ann finally gave in with a grudging "OK, go ahead, you've worn me down." Just in time, from my point of view, because if they had continued growing at the rate they had been, I couldn't have moved them myself, and both of us would have resented paying to have them moved.

They looked much better in their new position: on either side of another entrance to the west woods, a visual signal, like pillars, inviting you into the woods; and their blossoms were going to be acceptable from a distance. I performed the operation while Ann was hard at work revising one of her textbooks in a part of the house where she couldn't see what was going on. I had to maneuver two ten-foot shrubs with large root balls up a steep hill to their new positions in the upper lawn, remove the sod there, prepare the ground for them, install them, then lay the sod I had removed from the lawn over the filled-in holes where the shrubs had originally been growing. My first triumph was when for several days Ann didn't notice anything had changed, which I took to be a tribute at least to the cleanness of the operation. My second was when she did finally notice, saying that the view out of our bedroom and bathroom windows was much better than it had been.

Unfortunately, gardening, like any other human activity, has its failures, and the Roses of Sharon proved in the next year to be one of them. They didn't survive their first winter to act as the markers I had been pleased to provide for that entrance to the woods. I had probably cut off too many of their roots when I dug them up, or I hadn't watered them enough in subsequent weeks. There were other failures: only one of those five 'Pee-Gee' hydrangea transplants has survived. Deer chewed the other four year after year, which may have helped to weaken them, but the reason may have again been weakened roots. I don't know.

The biggest perennials I have moved are several ornamental grasses. These miscanthuses are magnificent plants, great green mounds getting taller and taller through the summer and fall, becoming perhaps even more beautiful in winter, when their flower heads fly like golden flags several feet above their golden leaves. But they keep spreading sideways too, and ours were overshadowing their smaller neighbors, gradually engulfing and eliminating them. I rescued some of the smaller neighbors by moving them, but four of the big grasses I moved to places where it didn't matter how much they dominated their neighbors: places where their powerful structural presence was needed much more than where they had been growing. But what a job: those root masses are hellishly dense and heavy, really tough to dig up, cut through, and divide. They now punctuate the two edges of a path through the meadow between the lower lawn and the line of fourteen weeping willows to its west, leading your eye down the path in the only straight line on the whole property. The meadow is very wet much of the year, and the grasses, which I thought would not mind the poor soil there, aren't yet as impressive as they had been, but we'll see. (I think the phrase I use most often when I garden is "We'll see.")

I have moved Siberian irises (they were big clumps too, and that was hard work, which has improved the original site and created a new site), and I have moved turtleheads, gooseneck loosestrife, daylilies, beebalm, artemisia, and coreopsis, all of them spreading too much for their own good and that of their neighbors. Then there were lamb's ears, rose campions, and mulleins filling niches all over the place with their furry gray rosettes. I decided to gather them in three separate but neighboring areas so they could make three collective patches of color instead of a lot of distracting dots here and there. The lamb's ears and rose campions worked out quite well, but the mulleins were a mistake. These were not those verbascum cultivars that look colorful in catalogues but the wild mulleins, which come up strong, tall, and showy in lousy soil, but in my prepared soil were a floppy, dreary, mess with only rather dirty hints of pale yellow for flowers.

I consider my most successful transplants to be the smallest: forget-me-nots generously given by Ruth and Leon; periwinkle dug from a very large patch under the trees at the side of our dirt road; pachysandra from around our big central weeping willow where it had been encroaching into the surrounding lawn; and ajuga from a garden it had been spreading over like a bright stain. All of these I moved to a large area that slopes up from the eastern edge of the lower lawn, getting afternoon sun under deciduous trees. I enjoyed the process, in each case moving a large number of individual plants. The periwinkle and pachysandra I dug out, and dug in, in clumps, but the ajuga plants I had to pull out of the areas they had invaded one by one on hands and knees, placing them in their new positions on hands and knees, standing back every so often to see how many square feet I was gradually filling in. That area, which I later called the east slope, became a garden of ground covers.

And so it goes. We are lucky enough to have the space to accommodate the plants, even the most invasive ones, that we need to move. What if our garden were much smaller, say, the size of the gardens my aunts created and looked after in England? Would I be moving plants as often as I am now? No, but I bet the amount of time I would devote to it, compared to doing all those other things that constitute gardening, would be roughly the same. Maybe I would change my mind more frequently than my aunts did.

In ungardened nature, plants generally grow from seeds in one spot and die in that same spot, and because nature abhors a vacuum and plants have a lot of exceedingly close neighbors, life for them is one long struggle. In the gardened world, plants are grown in one place, maybe a wholesale nursery, then moved perhaps to a retail nursery, then moved again to your garden or mine. Or you grow them in one spot of your garden and leave them there until they die. Or you grow them in one spot, then move them to another spot, then maybe to another, and another. Depending on the care with which you move them each time, life can be an improvement for them over life in nature or over life in one spot in a garden. That's what I hope, at any rate, as I carry on moving plant after plant. I hope I'm also improving the condition and the looks of each section of the property, and I hope I'm improving the condition and the looks of the property as a whole. We'll see.

CHAPTER 4

Digging in Clay

"OF ALL THE TECHNIQUES of gardening which are aimed to promote the general flourishing of plants, allow me to say what I personally believe is the truth, that nothing else is quite so important as digging, and giving the plant an earth of good texture to get started in." That's Henry Mitchell in "Dig It!" which is a section of his "Reflections on Gardening" in *The Essential Earthman* (1981). The importance of digging and making sure that the soil has good texture (or structure) is surely a truism, but I like Mitchell's good-humored three-page lecture because he makes it clear that it's a truth easily forgotten or ignored by anyone who is as lazy as he says he is. He knows he needs to rub the message in, and I know I need to have it rubbed in. You can't just jam the roots of a rose into a lawn like ours at Ginger and expect it to thrive. If you want to see good growth and beautiful blossoms next year, you're going to have to put in some physical labor and provide a more nurturing environment. Yes, I know. I just wish digging here were easier than it is.

Digging flowerbeds which have already been "improved" — that is, already dug and had compost or sand or other components added to make it easier for plants to spread their roots — is one thing. The ten small perennial beds we inherited are mostly like that, and digging them is a piece of cake. Digging the rest of our property, which is unimproved, is another thing entirely. We have a lot of lawn, so grass, weeds, and wildflowers don't mind the conditions there, but dig down anywhere under that greenery and you come to heavy clay on top of miserable-looking subsoil and, very quickly, hardpan. The clay topsoil seldom dries out (some years it never does), so digging it with a spade means lifting unbearably heavy sodden chunks upward with a squelching sound. When or if it does finally dry out, it becomes rock-hard, and digging it in that condition with a spade is equally impossible, like trying to get a knife through butter which has just come out of the freezer.

I am often tempted to extend our perennial beds into the lawn to make more of a show of them, and I often dream about starting new beds in the lawn or at its edge. But a new bed doesn't look like anything unless it's fairly large, and it can't begin to be a decent home for the sort of plants I would like to see in it without being thoroughly dug and improved. It's when I contemplate all that digging and improving that I start to feel lazy and find easier things to do.

I have bent a spade in our clay soil, which was not something I ever thought could happen. I retired it immediately and used instead a spade I had bought with a gift certificate, a tough shiny British-made tool which its maker describes as an heirloom. Its "forged by hand, heat-treated carbon steel is flexible enough to absorb shock," I read, and it won't "bend or break under pres-

sure." It won't bend — well, that's good; but still, pushing its blade into the ground with all my weight, getting
nowhere, then balancing on the top of the blade with
both feet and bouncing up and down to force it in is not
the way I want to work when there are a lot of square
yards to be dug. Also, when the blade is in at last, the
subsequent movement, of dislodging and lifting the
soil, wet or dry, is a serious threat to the back. And as for
double-digging (digging another blade-depth into the
subsoil), forget it, even with the king of spades.

But I have made new gardens in the lawn: one around
a young birch in the lower lawn, one under an apple tree
at the edge of the upper lawn near the kitchen, one on
the slope in the east woods I cleared for the groundcovers, and, most recently, a long thin crescent in the upper
lawn. How did I manage? I didn't use a spade. I used
one of my favorite gardening tools, a mattock. "A what?"
is the reaction I have come to expect when I mention
this tool. (I don't talk about it a lot, but it does come up
in conversation every now and again.) It has a shaft like
a pickax or sledgehammer, and its head has a blade on
each side of the shaft, one like a narrow ax, the other at
right angles to the shaft, like an adze. ("What's an adze?"
is the next question. It's a woodworking tool, shaped
like that part of a mattock.) The mattock is fairly heavy
to swing over your head, but you can get lots of momen-
tum on the downward swing, which drives the blade sat-
isfactorily deep into the soil. Then dislodging the clump
of soil, with any small accompanying rocks, is a relatively easy leverage action. A repeat swing can get you
down into the subsoil.

For the garden I started two years ago under the
apple tree near the kitchen, I used the adze side of this
wonderful tool to slice off the top couple of inches of

lawn, rolled up strips of sod as I moved backward, and consigned the rolls to the compost heap, then attacked the bared soil with the adze side again, turning to the ax side when I came across tree roots. I dumped wheelbarrow-loads of compost on the newly exposed soil, chopped and churned it all in with the mattock again, dumped loads of mulch on top of the mixture, and planted. The outcome in flowering perennials last year was disappointing after all that effort, but that was my fault and the fault of deer, not the fault of the mattock, which performed as always, just fine.

I thought that I was the only person to dig like this — Ruth and Leon don't, nor do Roberta and Viki — until Jill Gerrain, a professional gardener we play tennis with, with a powerful serve and a great overhead, told me she never uses anything else on tough soil. I wonder how many other gardeners with problem soil use mattocks. The catalogues that feature them don't mention their usefulness for digging in clay. The Brooklyn Botanic Garden publishes a very good series of small books for gardeners, a recent one being devoted to Essential Tools, with a section in which experts pick their six can't-live-without tools, but with no mention of, let alone enthusiasm for, my favorite tool. Is heavy clay rare among soils? I don't think so. Or do Jill and I know something about digging in clay that these folks don't? I doubt it. Or do these experts work only, or mostly, in improved soils? That could be it.

Human interaction with soil, improved or unimproved, is where horticulture starts (agriculture, too, of course). It's gardening's crucial moment, when we decide whether to break the skin of the earth at this particular point, have a look inside, maybe pull something out, maybe mix something in, maybe plant something there. Once I have made the elemental, almost existential decision and am committed to the act, I for one value digging as much as, perhaps more than, any of the other cleaner, easier gardening jobs, such as pruning, spraying, staking, or snipping flowers for the dinner table. And by digging I mean not only spading or forking improved beds, mattocking new beds, and planting large bulbs, all energetic jobs started in the upright position with a long tool, but also the much more intimate work of kneeling to plant and weed in the top few inches of soil with a small tool or bare fingers.

I have spent a great deal of time down there, with my face inches from the soil, examining it. What's going on in a handful of dirt? I have been told, and I believe, although I can't see them, that billions of bacteria and millions of fungi and protozoans are breaking down organic molecules in each cubic inch of topsoil into their mineral components, which are then soluble in water and soakable-up by the finest root hairs of living plants. I can't see all that activity, but I can see the worms, which digest decaying plant material and in the process provide organic molecules for the bacteria, fungi, and protozoans to break down and which compared to them are inconceivably gigantic. Ann says "Yuk!" when she sees a worm — and says a lot more than that, and worse, if she sees more than one — but the more of these long, blind, squirmy things I see, the better structured I know the soil is going to be, and the happier I am.

When I'm kneeling in the lawn or garden, I wear kneepads, one of the more essential items of clothing for this job and guaranteed to make Ann laugh and point. ("Where did you get those pan lids strapped to your legs?") I don't wear gloves because I can't feel through

them, and I need to feel, so by the evening my finger-
nails are broken and dirty. I dig out weeds and dig in
bleeding hearts, Lenten roses, and foamflowers in a garden east of the house; a number of different groundcovers on the east slope; narcissi in many different places.
It's a lot of down and dirty work, and a good tool is
as essential as good kneepads. I tried using a trowel.
"Crafted in England," says one of the leading makers of
trowels, "these long-lasting tools are made of carbon
steel coated with enamel, and smooth, strong ash han-
dles that resist splintering and protect against blisters."
But, guess what? In our clay, they bend. Yes, I have bent
every trowel I have owned except the "Handform" trowel
(probably called other things by different makers), an
ergonomic tool made of "extremely strong polycarbon-
ate engineering resin." I like this trowel, but it's not
sharp enough to dig into unimproved clay, so I use it
only where I use a spade, in our perennial beds.

In our unimproved clay I use my other favorite tool,
which some makers call a soil knife, others a farmer's
weeder, others a grub knife, yet others a gardener's
knife. ("It Digs, It Cuts, It Saws. A 3-in-1 tool you can't
live without!" And sure enough, it's one of the six tools
one of the experts in that Brooklyn Botanic Garden
booklet can't live without.) It's basically a dagger. "What
are you going to do with that thing?" Ann asked when it
arrived in the mail. Its point is sharp enough to penetrate heavy clay easily and it has a serrated edge. It digs
into the soil, then saws it so you can cut a cylinder of soil
quickly, and it doesn't bend. It's a tough little tool, it
feels much more like an extension of my hand than a
trowel ever did, and I use it the whole time.

Henry Mitchell finished his funny and wise piece on
digging with a little illustration, a nineteenth-century

drawing of a frog with a spade. The frog has its left foot on the left side of the spade's blade, and both its hands are resting on the top of the handle. The artist might also have shown the frog kneeling with a trowel in one hand and a small plant in the other. Those are our classic images of gardening, aren't they? Or if not of gardening, at least of digging? Yes, but that's not how I dig in clay. I grant that if the artist had given the frog soil like ours and portrayed it swinging a mattock wildly over its head to hack into the earth, great drops of sweat flying off its body into the margins of the page, or alternatively bending over and preparing to stab the earth with a dagger, readers might have been surprised, if not alarmed. But I would have said, "That's me. That's how I have to work around here." And Ann would have agreed.

 CHAPTER 5

Making Lists

"GARDENING": QUICK, what image comes to mind when you hear the word? A lady in a big straw hat and a long dress, with a basket of flowers in her left hand and pruners in her right, leaning over a long multicolored border of flowers on a sunny summer day? That's certainly a picture I recognize and like. It's a composite, planted in my mind as an ideal by numerous gardening magazines, garden supply catalogues, and plant catalogues, and its brilliant border represents something of what I am working toward. But the realistic picture of my gardening life is very different, and not only because I am male, Ann doesn't wear those sorts of clothes, and Ginger doesn't yet boast a border like that. Gardening for me is first of all labor of the sort that drenches me in sweat, gets my clothes filthy, and makes my arms, legs, and back ache — not a pretty picture. And second, gardening for me is also mental work, or rather, mental activity — thinking and wondering and worrying and planning — that could only be pictured unromantically as a man sitting at a desk, making lists.

As a list maker I am not in the same league as Ann, whose handbag is stuffed with so many lists that watching her search for the right one can be a tense experience. I make very few lists, but the lists I do make are an important part of my gardening. For five years I made two types, but I've recently come up with a third. One type is the one I jot down almost every day during spring, summer, and fall: a gardening "to do" list, including jobs like *"weed east slope garden, spray anti-deer stuff on hostas, prune white birch, edge front deck garden, water daylilies around white birch,"* and so on, with some of the items probably marked with a question mark. One of the great pleasures of my day is to come in in the evening, sit down with a drink, check off items on the list as the body aches diminish, and start compiling tomorrow's. (Sometimes I'll find my list with an item added to it at the bottom in a familiar hand not my own: *kiss wife,* for instance.)

The items on these daily lists are usually tactical and realistic, so it generally works out that what I plan to do in a day corresponds reasonably well with what I actually do, but not entirely. I'm not a professional working for clients or for a boss. Another of the great pleasures of my day is knowing that I can at any moment do something I hadn't thought of until a minute before instead of what I had thought of last evening.

My second type of list is strategic. I make it once or twice a year, and it's likely to include things that will change the place somewhat, like an annual business plan with larger goals than maintaining the status quo. The same thing applies to this list as to my daily lists: some things get done, and some don't. Here is one of these lists I made a couple of years ago.

- *Soil test.* I had attended a six-week class entitled "Soil Management." The course's climax was how to interpret the results of a soil test. Our soil here is heavy clay. I know that, but our teacher and the books tell me I should know how the soil varies in all the different parts I am working on, taking several samples from each. That's a big job, which I suppose I could break down into smaller ones: test the soil in a few areas first, see if the areas vary much, fix them (if they need fixing), and go on to other areas. But then there's the matter of the math involved. The course had been very well attended, held in a theater instead of a classroom, but as soon as the teacher told us that we needed to do some math to apply the results of a soil test to our buying of fertilizer, three quarters of the class groaned, including me. Anyway, I keep postponing this job, and the lazy part of me feels satisfied enough that the plants I am growing in most of the areas are not dying or even struggling. When they do struggle, I suspect it is because of inadequate light or shade or too much or too little moisture. But of course I can't be certain it isn't some component in the soil.

- *Improve path from car to front deck.* This is a stretch of sloping lawn which gets covered in snow in winter and which is difficult when it's icy. We would like it to be safer and easier for us and for guests. I keep postponing this, too, probably because Ann and I can't figure out what it should consist of and look like, and we keep wondering whether it is worth the trouble for a few bad weeks in the year.

- *Fix deck around pool.* The wood is rotting and becoming a hazard. A patch job would look awful, so we must replace the whole thing, which will be expensive. Then, do we want to keep the present design or instead have bluestone and grass? The need for this work has now become urgent, so we have to decide soon.

- *Plant garden east of house.* I did this. The area is the least visible part of the property, the utility part, with a propane gas tank up against the wall, service lines coming in overhead, and compost piles nearby. The strip of garden was shady and nondescript. Lilacs had grown so tall there that they were tangling with the electricity and phone lines and not flowering much, so I moved them, and now we have a garden I'm pleased with: a line of bleeding hearts at the back, hellebores in the middle, and foam flowers at the front. The foliage is attractive, particularly the bleeding hearts and the foam flowers, and they all flower for far longer than any other plant in the place.

- *Plant garden around west apple tree.* The magnificently shaped old apple was revealed when I started making an entrance into the west woods. I put daffodils under it, but then we couldn't mow the grass until their leaves died, so the area looked ratty. I have planted more daffodils and edged the area with stones, but I want the dying leaves of the daffodils to be hidden by perennials instead of straggly grass, and I haven't got around to that yet. Meanwhile, I have killed the grass and dumped a lot of mulch on the area, so it looks like a garden instead of just a problematic area of lawn. So the job is half finished.

- *Weed whacker.* The string kept getting knotted up in its cylinder, and it became such a hassle that I stopped using it. I wanted to just get it fixed, but then

I realized that I didn't much like it anyway, as it was heavy. I bought a lighter one, and have used it a lot. It too keeps getting knotted up, and rethreading the string is a drag, but the machine is extraordinarily useful. I need to do some research to find a better one.

- *Move weeping birch and river birch.* This item has a question mark against it. The trees are between the front of the house and the place where cars park. They are beautiful, but so is the crab apple very close to them, and the three are growing into one another. We probably should have moved these when we moved the other trees and the five hydrangeas at the front of the house, but we didn't, so we must do it now. We know where they would look good on their own: the weeping birch on the right of the driveway as you enter the property (on the left as you look down from the house to the entrance), and the river birch up in the top lawn. The approach to the front deck from the car (one of the items earlier in this list) should be easier when the weeping birch is gone.

- *Research lawn tractors.* I did this and ended up buying a secondhand golf cart, which has changed my gardening life. I used to have to haul compost and mulch by wheelbarrow from piles by the entrance, an uphill slog to most places on the property. Moving stones to create low edges to gardens I also had to do by wheelbarrow. Carrying stones or mulch or compost to the upper lawn was more than a slog, it was almost prohibitive. The golf cart climbs to the upper lawn easily and has enabled me to start a whole new garden up there (something that wasn't on any list).

- *Benches.* There were several places in the parklike

property that cried out for benches, so you could stop and sit and look around. We had two made for twenty-five dollars each and another for fifty. They worked well, but the twenty-five-dollar benches were rotting. On one of his visits from England, Roger designed and made two replacements. Upgrading other benches has remained an item on successive annual lists.

- *Improve meadow path.* The meadow, between the lower lawn and the west woods, is a feature of the property, and so is the path through it, the one straight line on our property if you except the buildings and the swimming pool area. I had moved some ornamental grasses to mark the sides of the path. I added more of the same, and will continue to do so.

- *Aerial photo.* Our friends David and Karen have one and I would like one, but the company that flies over and takes the photos quotes a high price, and I am making do with satellite photos from the Web.

- *Learn plants in lawn.* Our lawn isn't just grass, it's a lot of grasses, weeds, and wildflowers. I made a New Year's resolution to learn what they all are. It took me from lawn to reference book and back again a great many times, and I made progress, but I still have a lot to learn.

Looking at another, later, annual list, I see that I managed to do only half of the items on it, and not all of the jobs I did were successful. I *moved the lilacs,* and they have survived in their new position, but although I did *move the Roses of Sharon,* they didn't survive. I bought and planted *twelve baby trees* for a dollar each from the National Arbor Day Foundation, but none of them survived. I *fixed the garden west of the garage,* which had been a complete mess, but I could do more to improve it. I haven't finished *fixing the garden around the south bench,* and I still haven't figured out how to *improve the entrance to the property.*

And that's the way subsequent annual lists have worked out. Some of the jobs get done and some don't. So a couple of years ago I wondered: should uncompleted items go straight to the top of the next year's list? Did the fact that I never got around to them mean that I had not thought each of them through, had not, for instance, made a daily list of things I had to do to achieve each of them, or did it mean that they were not worth getting around to? So I thought that maybe I should compile yet a third type of list, which would amount to a long-term plan that would help prioritize the annual lists, making my work somewhat more organized.

Making that sort of list means having to address a question I was asked in our first years here and am still occasionally asked when I describe the place: what do I plan for it over the years? What's my vision? To which I used to reply: I'm not sure yet, I'm working on it. Not a satisfactory answer if I'm serious about what I'm doing. I tend not to think further ahead than a year or two or three, at the most, but of course three years is a short time in the lives of perennials and shrubs, and it's no time at all in the lives of trees, the dominant component of any garden. So I tried to think of what could be achieved over the course of a decade.

I never wrote out a long-term plan. What would I have done with it? Put it on the wall over my desk, with the framed reproduction of Dürer's watercolor of grasses? I don't take myself that seriously. But I did think about it, and I still think about it. There are indeed some underlying ideas that guide what I am doing; there is even one big general aim that could serve as the equivalent of a mission statement accompanying the plan. If I ever wrote it out, it would be one sentence: *I want anyone who comes onto our property to like what they see enough to be happy to come back.* That's very general, committing me only to presenting something good-looking to anyone who comes to our place at any time. I do want service people, delivery people, and other new visitors to continue over the years to look around and say, "Nice spot you have here."

But I also want the place to improve continually on the status quo, and it's the individual items in the hypothetical long-term plan which would commit me to some directions for improvement. Here's one: *I want people to perceive that our nine and a half acres are all "garden."* Half of our acreage is woods, much of the rest is lawn, parklike, and there are now fifteen perennial beds. I want people to see that they are all integrated, especially the woods and the open area. For example, from the most central point, the house, you see the perennial beds nearby and some perennial beds in the middle distance, and across the lawn you see the woods in the distance, the largest area of which is to the west. I want people to want to go into the west woods. That means I have to make it obvious where to enter them without having to actually walk toward them to figure it out, and that means either some system of paths or a system of plant or artificial markers, or both.

Another very basic aim: *I want individual small gardens to be memorably full of color at least once a year.* I would like to photograph Ann surrounded by gloriously colorful flowers in a number of different places. Two, perhaps three, of our gardens at present are fairly full and fairly colorful in midsummer, but they don't compare to the one in that ideal composite picture we have in our minds after leafing through magazines and catalogues, and the other gardens are relatively weak and need boosting.

I want each area of the property to be visually interesting from a distance and close to. But wait a minute: am I being too ambitious? Any one of these three items could give rise to more annual lists than I have working years left. Each area? There are a lot of areas. There's the upper lawn, the lower lawn, the meadow, the swimming pool area, several quite different sections of border between lawn and woods, the west woods, the east woods — it goes on and on. Am I crazy to think of committing to all this?

At this point I should console myself by thinking of things I don't have to be bothered with. A list would include:

- *Vegetables.* There's no question: a home-grown tomato is one of the joys of life, ditto a home-grown strawberry, but let them bring joy to Roberta and Viki, who fenced in a patch a couple of years ago and grow excellent tomatoes, wonderful zucchinis, basil, and a long list of other eatables in it. There was a large "kitchen garden" at Acaster, and Aunt P had her vegetable garden and my uncle his fruit cage, but that type of gardening is a whole different type of gardening from mine, and I'm not going to get into it.

- *A greenhouse.* The best tomatoes I have ever eaten were taken warm off the vine in greenhouses in England when I was a kid, but I'll leave greenhouse gardening to Roger, who has recently built a greenhouse for his wife, Jenny, at Acaster, and they are growing flowering plants in it. I'm eager to hear reports of their successes, but I'm not going to join them in that type of work.

• *Plants that can't grow in our hardiness zone.* I would love to grow gardenias, calla lilies, and orchids, but I can't, so they are very low on my priority list of plants to even learn about. When Ann shows me a picture of a wonderful plant in a magazine and suggests we grow one, I immediately check out its hardiness zone. Sorry, no camellias this far north. My reading of magazines is very selective for the same reason. I have too little time as it is to learn about all the plants that can grow in zone 5.

• *Plants that can't grow in clay.* We have heavy clay, so exactly the same applies to all the plants that won't grow in clay. I would be wasting precious time and space if I tried to grow them at Ginger, so I don't even try to remember their names.

• *Flat land.* Our land slopes, so many formal design schemes and features would look odd here or wouldn't work. No need to consider them.

• *Views into the distance.* Ann likes trying to see the Berkshires from the top of our upper lawn, and I think she wishes we could see more of them. But we can't, so it's not something to worry about. We have plenty of seventy-five-yard-long views within our own property.

• *Running water.* There's something magical about the look and sound of trickling water, but the closest we come to a stream on our property is a ditch which gurgles after big rains, but seldom dramatically enough and never long enough to be an attractive feature or to provide waterfalls or to feed water-loving plants. Most of the year it's dry and unattractive. Maybe trying to improve its look should go onto an annual list.

- *Water features,* such as fountains or ponds with waterlilies. We have a swimming pool, a very different thing, not plant-friendly at all. Adding formal water features or a pond would look odd anywhere near it.

- *Topiary.* I'm not interested in this sort of gardening, nor knot gardens, nor labyrinths. Too labor-intensive, too precious.

That makes me feel a bit better. Not having to worry about all those things should free up plenty of mental time. Then there are items that I can't afford, such as a big, strong *deerproof fence* around the perimeter of our property. Another big item that we may try to afford is an *extension to our drive* that would allow more cars to park here and turn around easily. This item could possibly go on an annual list. *Drawing and painting plants,* on the other hand, which I would love to learn to do and which I believe would be truly helpful in learning about plants, is too big a job, so I will stick to photographing them.

Which reminds me that one of my annual list items, only partially completed, was to get to know all the plants in our lawn. Well, I would certainly want a long-range plan to include an extension of that item. *I want to know the identity of all the plants on our property, including trees, shrubs, wildflowers, weeds, and all perennial species and varieties.* Isn't this as basic a piece of knowledge about a place as its hardiness and heat zone, the amount of sun it gets, and the nature of its soil? Isn't it perverse to want to know what *might* grow here when I don't yet know what *does* grow here?

Maybe the long-term list should be kept to four items: those three items I started with, plus the last one I just thought of. So it would be: *integrate the whole; make each garden colorful once a year; make each area interesting from a distance and close to; and identify all plants.* What I notice is that I am not planning to make drastic changes to the whole, like getting rid of the swimming pool or starting a fifty-yard perennial border. In our house, Ann and I follow an aesthetic of accretion, changing things quite slowly, finding that the rooms reflect our story together over the years, not the inherited design of previous owners nor the new design of someone else or our own one-moment vision. I think that's the best way for me to view the future of our garden too. Before and after photographs of the garden, if I remember to take them, will show how much I have changed it in any five years. It's going to turn out to be a huge amount, I know, even though month by month it won't seem to be changing much. Progress will be gradual, one sweaty job at a time.

CHAPTER 6

Smelling the Roses

STOP AND SMELL THE ROSES: it's an appealing way to suggest how a harried executive, say, should take a break every now and then to enjoy some of the simple pleasures of life, if only for a moment. "Ah yes!" the tycoon would think, bending over a bunch of roses, "This is what it's all about. When did I last do this? Life would be better if I did this more often." I couldn't agree more with the general idea, or with the particular activity suggested.

As far as I can remember, no one has ever suggested that I stop and smell the roses, and I mean to keep it that way. Maybe there are some gardeners who spend so much time *working at* their garden that they need to be told to take a break and enjoy it, but I find it hard to imagine. And I can't think anyone will ever tell me to do it literally either — "Hey, James, where are you going? Stop right there and smell those roses," in a Botanic Garden, for instance, when I might appear to be going too fast past the 'Crimson Glories'. No, it's much more likely that I would go straight for the roses, come close to their blooms, and inhale deeply through the

nostrils with a sigh of bliss and ever-renewed amaze-
ment. Gardening can be a lot of hard physical work, but
what's it for if not to revel in the perfect shape or scent
(or taste, if you are a vegetable gardener) of what you
have been laboring to grow?

Ann never tells me to stop and smell the roses. She
never stops to smell the roses herself. It's not that she
doesn't know how to relax: she's great at it. And it's
not that she doesn't like roses: she loves them. No, she
doesn't smell roses or any other flower, in our garden or
anywhere else, because she worries that if she does she
will start sneezing. I too worry that she will, so I don't
tell her to smell them. She sneezes louder than anyone
I know. We both have only to set foot in a store which
sells scented candles before we are outside again, cursing. Our noses start twitching as soon as someone with
powerful perfume sits next to us on the subway. But
when it comes to flowers, Ann is more allergic than I
am. It makes me sad, because the words "intensely fragrant" are words I specifically look for in a plant catalogue, but they make Ann pull a face.

One of the best ways to appreciate the beauty of an
individual flower is to cut it and put it in a vase on the
dining room table. But I have to be careful about what
flower I bring. If Ann is going to start sneezing while
we take our first drink at dinner, the enjoyment of flower,
drink, and meal is spoiled. Ann likes a rose when it's
still a bud and I like it then too, but on the whole I prefer it when it has just opened out. However, I'm happy
to cut a bud for the table because at that stage its fragrance is not yet at its strongest and we can both admire
it for a short time. When it opens, I point out how much
better it looks, and Ann tries to win the argument by
reaching for a handkerchief and threatening a huge sneeze.

There's another plant that, like the rose, can deliver some of the most perfect flowers, in shape and fragrance, imaginable. It's the lily. But that's only my opinion, which happens not to be shared by my spouse. If I had my way, I would plant masses of these gorgeous things all over our property. I think the colors, textures, and shapes of their petals, the brazen exhibitionism of their protruding stamens, and their heady fragrances are the height of desirable sensuality. Ann has nothing against sensuality, but she thinks lilies look artificial and smell of burned plastic. In our never-ending argument over whether to buy more of these wonderful plants, she is helped, unfortunately, by the fact that lily buds appear to be the items that animals like to eat first in our garden. No sooner is a promising shoot out of the ground than — *munch, munch, munch,* in the middle of the night — it's gone, which makes these plants the most annoying I can think of to grow. (Tulips are eaten as soon as they appear too; they are not fragrant at all, and beautiful though they are, they aren't as beautiful as lilies — my opinion only — so I don't even try to grow them.)

Roses can be very annoying. Their blooms may look wonderful, but the plants often look terrible. We have four deep red roses whose names I don't know, each in a different garden; three pale pink 'New Dawn' roses, which climb on the fence around our swimming pool; three pink roses ('The Fairy') by the side of wooden steps down to the swimming pool; and a pink and white striped rose, whose name I don't know, climbing on the railing of our front deck. We inherited all of these from the previous owners of our property — I would know all their names if I had planted them myself — and each is annoying in one way or another. But we also have a lot of *rugosa* roses given to us last year, as roots and judiciously pruned stems, by Ruth and Leon, and I feel more optimistic about these.

'New Dawn' is a popular winner of numerous awards. It certainly wins, hands down, in the competition for most vigorous plant on our property (mint is runner-up), which would be fine if it didn't also win in the viciousness competition (well, after poison ivy). Every spring I see 'New Dawn's' bark has been shredded by some animal and many canes are dead, so I cut it back drastically, a job I hate doing. Yards and yards of densely prickled stems claw at my clothes and skin, puncturing them and clinging tight. Pulling the prickles out invariably allows other prickles to grab hold, and the more blood I see the more I wonder, is this really worth it?

It's a question that this rose provokes at other seasons too. The 'New Dawns' are tied to a fence around our swimming pool, and they grow so quickly through the fence into the area where swimmers and sunbathers walk that I have to cut them back again and again. I suppose I shouldn't blame the plant, which is doing what it has to do. The problem is obviously one of positioning. But then the flowers, which smell pretty good, are the garden's strongest magnet for Japanese beetles, so the pleasure of inhaling their scent at close range (which Ann wouldn't do anyway) is likely to be mixed with disgust. I wonder again, what's the point?

The deep red roses, which look and smell wonderful, 'The Fairy' roses, which smell a little and can look good, and the pink and white striped rose, which looks good but doesn't smell at all, all suffer from black spot. I think that any plant that loses all its leaves in late summer, becoming a network of naked canes, barely rates consideration as a garden plant, even if it has produced wonderfully formed buds and flowers a few weeks before, which these do. I resent having to consider spraying any plants in our garden in order to keep their leaves on. Lavender looks great and smells wonderful, and it doesn't lose its leaves. It smells so good, in fact, when your legs brush against it on a hot summer day that even Ann loves it — she doesn't have to bend and sniff it. She likes the smell of our lilacs for the same reason. So why do we put up with roses, which are beautiful one month and ugly the next, and scratch us, and attract Japanese beetles?

Their flowers are just so seductive. Singly or in a bouquet, roses are romantic. If you asked people quickly to name a flower, I bet most would say "rose." Roses are the essence of flower. A rose is a rose is a rose. Except that it isn't. There are an intimidating number of different *types* of rose and thousands of different cultivars, each bred to be the perfect rose, and none quite managing to be so, as, for instance, plenty of narcissi have managed, in my opinion, to be the perfect narcissus. (Although, come to think of it, narcissi don't look so great when their leaves have not yet died, but that's different.) Some lavenders are perfect lavenders. Anyway, Henry Mitchell, who writes so well about roses, as about everything else in the garden, says, in "Thinking about Roses" (in *The Essential Earthman*):

> Everybody would agree (except those who make it a point of honor never to agree with anything) that roses should be healthy, beautiful in individual flower, highly fragrant, constantly in flower during the warm seasons of the year, blessed with ornamental foliage, and possessed of overall grace. The trouble is there are no roses, none, that do not fail in one or more of these

desirable qualities. So the choice comes down to this: since no rose is perfect, which imperfections will you accept, and which qualities will you regard as indispensable?

My indispensable criteria would be deer resistance, pest resistance, disease resistance, beauty of individual flowers, intense fragrance, and overall grace. Ann's would be much the same, but she would include constant flowering and would drop fragrance. Our roses produce good-looking flowers, but otherwise they don't measure up.

The *rugosas* will not be perfect either; I know that. They will attract deer and Japanese beetles, they will be exceedingly prickly, they will not be in constant flower, and their flowers will not be outstanding. But their flowers will be delightful, their leaves will be ornamental, and their flowers *and their leaves* will be fragrant. They will be disease-resistant and tough, I believe, to the point of indestructibility. And they will grow into the sort of large, dense shrubs that will be perfect for their site, at the bottom of our lower lawn, where they can act as a screen, where Japanese beetles won't be so visible, and where their prickliness will be an asset.

I will feel good if I can grow ours as well as Ruth and Leon have grown theirs. I thrust them into our heavy clay rather unceremoniously last fall with a little compost. They lost all their leaves immediately, as Ruth said they would, but then they sprouted more leaves, to my great relief. I look forward to seeing them grow big in two or three years. I'm counting on it, although I plan to do very little for them. They are on their own down there. I wonder how much tender loving care the *rugosas* in the local supermarket's parking lot get. They are in great shape. I admire them every time we shop there, provoking a sigh from Ann when I slow down to look at them as we drive in and eye-rolling every time I walk over to them with the shopping cart to inspect them closely. Anyway, when ours do grow big and strong (when, not if), you can be sure that I will take regular breaks from whatever I am doing in the garden to go over and smell them.

PROJECTS

CHAPTER 7

Walking in the Woods

IN OUR FIRST TWO YEARS at Ginger, I spent a great deal of time in the west woods. When I wasn't moving plants around (starting in our second year) or working through lists of general maintenance jobs I had given myself the evening before, I was in the west woods. I think Ann and Emily and Lucy and some of our friends and acquaintances were a bit puzzled when they saw how many hours I was spending out there. Wasn't I going to be *gardening* at Ginger? Hadn't I said that gardening was what I particularly wanted to do? Well, after those first two years, I did spend much more of my time tending to the various areas of the property that family and friends would call gardens: that is, the well-defined, unshaded or partly shaded areas planted with perennials and shrubs that promised flowers in spring, summer, or fall. In fact, since those first two years I have spent relatively little time in the west woods. (Working on the slope in the east woods came later.) But if asked what my most successful gardening has been, I would say it remains the project that I started in the west woods in those first two years. It isn't finished yet (how many gardening jobs ever are?), but it has already been successful, and it has also provided, among other things, one of the happiest days of my life.

When we bought the property, the half of it that was woods, and especially the four-acre section on the west side of the open area, was a particularly powerful attraction to me. For Ann, the woods provided the seclusion we both liked, but they were not the place she would be inclined to walk in unless it was easy sauntering. If it was remotely challenging, why would she bother, when there was so much pleasant lawn to walk on? For me, walking in woods, even fighting through them, is at least as moving an experience as walking around a beautifully designed flower garden, provided that there are places for me to stop every so often to look around. All those trees towering above, sometimes totally still and silent, at other times a pandemonium of noise and movement. There's not so much variety of color and scent among them as in a flower garden, but there's much more mystery and power, and I get a huge kick out of feeling awed.

It was clear that the previous owners were like Ann, only more so. They had certainly "gardened": their advertisement in the newspaper had mentioned the perennial gardens as a feature of the property, and they knew the Latin names of all their perennials and shrubs. But when I asked them about their woods, they looked surprised, shrugged as they confessed total ignorance, and changed the subject. For them the woods were a backdrop for the gardens, and nothing more. I got Ann to venture into them with me within hours of our ownership, and as soon as we had struggled a few feet into their shade, we knew that the previous owners had never, ever done what we were doing now. The weeds and shrubs and vines at the edge had grown so vigorously that they were a densely tangled thicket. Just behind this natural barrier was an artificial one, an electric fence, which the previous owners had paid someone to install: three wires threaded from three bright yellow insulators hammered into the trunk of a tree to three more bright yellow insulators hammered into another tree twenty yards away in one direction and the same in the other direction. The open "gardened" area was surrounded on all sides by overgrown weedy shrubs, in the south and north amounting to not much more than a thick hedge, in the east backed by fifty yards or more of trees, in the west by four acres of trees, everywhere a pleasant green screen in summer, but everywhere concealing, several feet back from the lawn, three lines of dirty silver.

The fence, zigzagging from tree to tree, parallel in places, in others sagging or missing, had been totally ineffective. Deer were all over the property. The previous owners had pointed apologetically to the line of what we would have recognized as hostas had they been allowed to keep their glossy wide leaves but were now nothing but a line of stem stubs in the soil. But if the wires had not deterred deer, they would certainly deter Ann. As she maneuvered her legs awkwardly over one wire while crouching under another and muttered, "Oh God, are we going to have to do this every time we go into the woods?" I knew that if I wanted her to walk in the woods, I was going to need all my powers of persuasion to get her to come with me.

I hate what hungry deer do to the plants on our property, particularly the perennials or shrubs or small trees I have bought or nurtured, but (and I have to argue this out with myself every time I see the branch tips of a little tree chewed off or that same line of hostas munched despite the smelly liquid I had sprayed all over it) I would rather surrender a percentage of our plants every year to deer than have ugly wires preventing me from walking easily through our own woods.

But it wasn't just that I wanted to be able to walk easily through the woods and not just that I wanted Ann to be able to walk easily there. I wanted the woods to welcome us. I wanted Ann *to want to* walk through the woods.

So one of my first acts as a gardener of our new property was to clamber and squeeze and thrust my way through the honeysuckle and weedy dogwood, wrench out those ugly yellow insulators with an iron bar, collect yards and yards of wire, and haul a trunkload off to the dump. Now at least the barriers to our walking on our own property were natural.

What was the experience I wanted Ann to share with me? Not wilderness: we could never kid ourselves that our few acres were that, although if we had a hundred times the number of acres I would indeed want to preserve a lot of them as an approximation of wilderness. Central Park in New York City has 843 acres, 35 of which are the wild-seeming Ramble, where I liked to eat lunch when I worked nearby, but the Ramble is of course not wild at all but planned and designed artfully with paths and benches. Roger's Stub Wood, 50 acres of his 500-acre farm, is "ancient woodland" but has roads all through it. But even in the Ramble and in Stub Wood, you can briefly wonder where you are, a momentary jolt of excitement.

Getting really lost in deep woods is one of the things everyone should experience at least once. (I'm not talking jungle, of course.) For a time you become what you had forgotten you always were and always will be, a human animal. Trees all around you, no buildings in sight, no paths, no sounds of traffic (unless maybe occasionally the sound of an airplane). No sounds of people. Silence, or the sounds of birds, and occasionally the sounds of other animals. You start looking forward to being a person again, with a name. Then that sudden thought: "Will I get back for the next meal?" Well, no one would ever have to experience that sort of worry in our few acres.

You can go for a walk to experience "nature" in a number of different ways. On a simplified scale, nature can be, starting at the near end, so to speak, a manicured, formal garden. Moving along the scale, it can be a semiformal garden; an informal garden; a wild garden; further on the scale it can be a woodland garden; familiar woods; unfamiliar woods; and finally at the far end of the scale it can be wilderness. At the near end of the scale we are relaxed and comfortable, accompanied always by the mind of the designer. At the far end of the scale we are on our own, exploring or lost, perhaps scared. I wanted to provide an experience somewhere between the middle of the scale and the far end. I wanted our few acres to provide a minute fraction of the pleasure afforded by the Ramble, where you can't see buildings or hear traffic and it's possible briefly to feel lost. I wanted our woods to become more familiar than that, and I wanted them to be seen as an integral part of a unified nine-and-a-half-acre "garden" — one of the items of my long-term plan — while at the same time being utterly unlike other parts of the garden, the lawn and the perennial beds.

Walking easily in our woods would mean not having to squeeze through those shrubs growing into one another, not having to push branches out of our way at every step, not having to look down continually to be sure of our footing. Our woods needed at least one entrance and at least one path. But where to get in, and where to walk?

I fought my way through the tangle of live and dead trees and shrubs, up and down, backward and forward, to find out what these woods had to offer, whether in fact a walk in them would be worthwhile. In one two-acre area, roughly the top part of the four-acre woods, there was a stand of eighty-foot white pines, with four or five oaks the same height, and four or five maples that height too, and at one corner of this area was a conspicuous outgrowth of rock, the highest spot on the property. Those two acres held the most promise for an interesting walk.

The likeliest place for a way into this area was conveniently near the house, and perhaps it had been an entrance into the woods a couple of decades ago. There was a dense border of sumacs, honeysuckle, briars, and weedy dogwood, behind which I could see a collapsed stone wall and a ditch on the other side of the wall; but at this particular spot the wall was so low that you hardly had to lift your feet to step over it, and the ditch was not very deep or wide. I started chopping and hacking and lopping, pulling and heaving, sawing and chain-sawing. I lopped brambles six feet high and wide, branch by arching branch, until I reached their central stems, which I cut at the base. Then I dug out the roots. The same with the honeysuckles (*Lonicera tartarica,* amazingly invasive, my enemy), which had grown up to ten feet tall, up to twelve feet wide, with six-inch, even nine-inch-diameter trunks at the base. The sumacs, fifteen feet high but with weak hollow stems, could be pulled up or dug out.

The numerous weedy dogwoods (*Cornus racemosa*) were grouped in congested clumps, but each individual was fairly small. A pile of sawed trunks, lopped branches, and scrub grew taller and taller as a narrow way into the woods gradually became an entrance. Whenever I walked into the house, having left my filthy clothes outside, Ann looked at the scratches on my face and arms and the bruises on my legs and said, "You've been out there in the woods again, haven't you?"

I was seldom anywhere else after I had breached that outer wall of vegetation. The first thirty feet of shrubs and young trees at the edge of the woods, with access to sunlight, had grown lush and impenetrable. Farther into the shade, the plants were smaller and weaker, but I was still measuring progress one square yard at a time. Honeysuckles my size I pulled and pushed until their roots gave way, sometimes sending me flying to the ground. Dead white pine branches stuck out twelve feet from their trunks at all angles, starting almost at ground level. Shrubs with half-inch-diameter stems were growing only two feet apart from one another. Small trees twenty feet tall with two-inch-diameter trunks were growing close enough for their branches at my height to be intertwined. You couldn't see the wood for the trees and shrubs.

I liked the idea of putting a bench on that rock at the high point of the two-acre area. It would feel good to sit there admiring the big white pines and glimpsing, through them, the lawn I had just left. I started clearing a path from the entrance up to the rock, and soon it took shape: ninety yards long, between ten and twenty feet wide, with a gentle curve in the middle dictated by the position of the big trees on either side.

In the winter I was up at dawn. If there was snow on

the ground, I could still lop or saw the branches poking sideways at me. In the spring I was out in the woods before dawn, listening for the first bird to start up, then cutting and clearing to the sound of hundreds of birds as the sky lightened. In the summer I was sweating so much by breakfast time that I had to make my first of several daily changes of clothes. Three piles of wood grew as I labored into the evening.

Roger flew from Acaster to stay with us for two weeks in the first summer, and in that short time much of the look of the area took shape. He knows woods. His Stub Wood (singular in England) is more than ten times the size of our woods, and he has done a huge amount of work in it. Within days of his arrival he had exposed and rebuilt the low wall, erected pillars of stone on either side of the gap in the wall to signal that this was indeed an entrance, chain-sawed the trunk of a huge dead elm that had fallen across what had become the path to the rock, and constructed a simple flat wooden bridge across the ditch. We were in the woods from dawn to dusk. "Boys with toys," Ann said.

When Roger left, I cleared between all the large trees in the two-acre area. I had wanted to saw and lop off all the dead branches to way up at the top, where the living branches would be left reaching across to one another like criss-crossing ribs in a Gothic cathedral's vault. My telescoping lopper couldn't reach more than a quarter of that distance, even at full extension, but the ground was soon covered with branches of all sizes, including some the size of trees. One fell so hard that it bounced up and gashed my hand, which needed twelve stitches in the hospital emergency room. Three piles of small trees and branches gradually became massive mounds, and I dragged more branches to form a sort of wall at the bottom of the cleared two acres. The two acres below this I planned to leave untouched.

The next year I pulled all the branches out of those three piles (which, as I looked through the woods, had become eyesores) to build up the wall at the bottom. I used the tree trunks in the piles to line the sides of the path up to the rock, on each side linking the big trees, so the growing tree trunks became giant fence posts. At the end of the path I placed a simple bench on the rock. When I got tired, I sat there and looked at the huge trees and through them. They were clear of competing and obstructive undergrowth for the first time in many years.

I particularly liked an area of open ground, surrounded by fifteen fine pines. I decided to link these trees at ground level with tree trunks, as I had the trees on either side of the path. When I did so, I found that the trunks on the ground formed the circumference of an almost perfect circle fifty feet in diameter. I left two small gaps in the circumference, one an entrance from the new path, and the other directly opposite, an exit. I put the thick, squat elm logs Roger had chain-sawed on either side of the entrance and on either side of the exit.

In one sense, the sense my family and friends agree on, all this work wasn't exactly gardening. I hadn't planted a thing. I had instead killed a great many plants. No, I wasn't creating a woodland garden. (That will take a very long time, if I am ever tempted.) But it was gardening in another sense, and it still is, as a work in progress. If I ever manage to integrate the open area with the woods so well that movement from one to the other is completely natural, then I think I will have gardened successfully. Recently I moved some tall decorative grasses (*Miscanthus*) from a garden near the house (a heavy, sweaty job) to places in the upper lawn, on either side of the two stone pillars at the entrance to the woods, to act as additional markers, but they are still not enough. As you look around from the open area, you notice that entrance, yes, but you still feel that the property is divided in two, one half open, the other woods, and I am not sure yet how to achieve the integration I want.

But judged by other standards, whether it is gardening or not, the work has been a huge success. For one thing, Ann goes for walks in the woods on her own, without any suggestion from me, let alone coaxing. For another, when Emily told us that she was going to get married, she also told us that she wanted to get married in the woods. So on the best day in her life, and one of my happiest, she had drinks and hors d'oeuvres set out on the top lawn; electrical cable laid into the woods for music at the ceremony; and on the lower lawn, after softball and Frisbee, she had dinner and dancing in a tent. It was a clear, hot summer day, and there was noise from early afternoon to early the next morning. For the ceremony, Emily had guests file between Roger's stone pillars, over Roger's bridge, into the cool of the woods, and into the circle. Then she and Dave walked through us all to the hushed music of two guitars and exchanged vows by the thick squat elm logs.

CHAPTER 8

Learning the Lawn

WHEN I AM DESCRIBING Ginger to people, I tend to concentrate on what I think they are likely to be most interested in, that is, the house, the perennial beds, and perhaps the fact that there is a swimming pool. I do say that half of the property is woods and that there is a lot of sloping lawn, but I tend to leave it at that.

But as a gardener, that's not the way I think about the property. I think of the woods as two different places: the west woods being larger than the east and less easy to see into. I think of the west woods itself as two different places: one the cleared area where Ann and I walk and where Em got married, and the other the area I have deliberately left uncleared, where Ann never walks. And I think of the east woods also as having two distinct sections: one, the very visible slope I have cleared and planted with groundcovers, and the other, the uncleared area between our house and the house of our nearest neighbor above us.

Similarly I think of the lawn as the upper lawn and the lower lawn. The upper lawn rises steeply behind the house and then levels off, so the top part is not visible from the house, while the lower lawn, which is much larger than the upper lawn, spreads out like a fan, widest at the bottom. And the lower lawn has itself three distinct parts: the part between the house and the drive, with several small specimen trees and shrubs in it; the mowed area below the drive, with a few trees in it; and the one acre which is so damp that it gets cut only once a year, if that, so it's meadow.

Then there is the strip of woods at the top of the property, which is nothing more than a thin short line of trees and shrubs between us and a neighbor's field, and the much thicker and longer strip at the bottom of the lower lawn, screening us from the road.

Furthermore, there is another large distinct area that is very easy to overlook but which I think about, namely the transition area at the edge of the woods, which I have cleared of briars and honeysuckle in several places, allowing wildflowers to come in. This ungardened transition area is itself different in different parts of the property, depending on the quality of the light it receives and on how long it has been left untouched. One part is full of pink, white, and purple wild phlox at one time of the year, then later full of white snakeroot, another part full of goldenrod late in the year.

As for the perennial beds, it goes without saying that they are quite distinct from one another, in quite different places, with different shapes and different plants arranged differently in each, and it also goes without saying that I am happy that they should be the focus of my and other people's attention. But gardening for me is much more than focusing on those beds. It's also figuring out what their role and the role of all the other parts should be in the larger picture. Should I enlarge the bed of daylilies around the raised lilac bed? Should

I divide the Siberian irises in the bed around the swimming pool shed and start a new iris bed with the extra plants in the middle of the upper lawn? How should I mark the entrance to the west woods at the bottom of the path through the meadow?

There are two parts that I don't have to think about — the uncleared areas of woods. I want them to remain precisely as we inherited them. The uncleared acre of the west woods is separated from the cleared area by the barrier I made from the branches and small trees I dragged from the cleared area. I walk through the uncleared area only very occasionally, and it's a whole different experience from anywhere else on the property: darker, more steeply sloped, and more of a struggle. The other part, in the east woods, slopes up between our house and our neighbors' house. This can fill out as much as it wants, to act as a baffle and screen.

I want to handle each part in such a way that the whole is visually integrated, the first item in my long-term plan. I guess this is where gardening becomes landscape design. And for me it entails, for a start, getting to know each part, and, more specifically, getting to know what lives in each part, which is another item in my long-term plan. And I guess that is where gardening becomes natural history.

I have, for instance, spent as much time working on the lawn as I have in the west woods. But my work on the lawn hasn't been the physical labor it was in the west woods. I don't even mow the lawn myself. The Callander team drives in with three or four machines and spends a couple of hours roaring backward and forward riding them or walking behind them, then weed-whacking the less accessible places, then blowing the edges clean. Ann and I don't mind the racket, knowing how good the place will look when they are through. When we notice it's all quiet again, we go out to admire the smooth surface of the lawn and breathe in the smell of cut grass.

But when it is wet, Callander's can't mow, and often they can't mow for a week or even two or three weeks, so the grass grows high, and so do all the other plants in the lawn, which is when I go to work. A few years ago I started trying to identify what was in the lawn, another part of my long-term plan.

Not long ago Ann and I saw some remarkable examples of lawn in an Arizona resort hotel where she was talking about one of her books at her publisher's spring sales conference. Flying from New York to Arizona is to stay in the same country and visit another world. The hotel's landscaping included massive saguaro cactuses, prickly pear, cholla and golden barrel cactuses, ocotillos, and paloverde trees, all of which would have been growing right there in the desert before the resort was built. But in one spot, at the entrance to a luxurious health spa, was a flat expanse of vegetation that in desert conditions would have been a mirage: a perfectly mown, bright green expanse of lawn. This cliché of modern American cultivation was both incongruous, surrounded as it was by genuine desert vegetation, and totally appropriate, serving as a sort of sensual introduction to the pampering treatments offered within. We wanted immediately to take off our shoes and sink our bare feet into its soft carpet. Ann pointed at it and said, "Why can't our lawn look like that?"

Later in the same resort we came across a bowling green, a perfectly flat rectangle, mown so low that we recognized immediately how appropriate the standard comparison is, to the felt of a billiard table. I got in the first word this time: "Don't say it, Ann. We can't do that. Our lawn is a whole different deal."

For a start, our lawn slopes so dramatically behind the house that when the Callander guys mow it, they balance by leaning away from their machines like small-craft yachtsmen in a high wind. Underlying rocks break the surface of our lawn in many places, threatening the blades of the machines above them. The rocks are the tops of boulders far too massive to move, without being quite high enough above the surface to offer interesting landscaping opportunities. The soil of our lawn is heavy clay on top of stuff our septic tank maintainer and excavator dismissed as "garbage," and after a rain it stays so wet that the mowers can't mow for a long time without leaving great gouges instead of alternate stripes of light and dark green. They try not to let the grass grow higher than four inches but often have to wait until it has grown to six inches or more. Several times they have had to wait until it was a meadow more than twelve inches deep.

One section of the lower lawn below the swimming pool is flat enough for us to play croquet when it's dry, but ours is a very different game from the one people play in that Arizona resort, where balls roll across green felt and keep rolling. On our lawn, the balls nestle half hidden in the grass, and hitting them hard enough to make them struggle through it for a few yards is an effort. One year a deer thought our lawn had long enough grass for its newly born fawn to feel protected — ten yards from our front door.

Finally, our lawn has a large number of plants besides grass. Most of them are inconspicuous most of the time, and I'm happy to see them flourish there. Some draw attention to themselves and I want to kill them.

But many are beautiful when you look closely at them, and I couldn't kill them for the same reason I couldn't kill that fawn, even though it will grow to eat some of our prize shrubs and perennials. The fact is, our lawn will never look remotely like either of those Arizona lawns, even if we wanted it to. Our lawn could use some improvements here and there, but overall we like it the way it is.

At least it is green most of the year. In fact, it stays green longer than other lawns around here in the summer and it stays white longer than other lawns in the winter, presumably because it's a north-facing slope, so it stays cooler, and its heavy clay holds moisture longer after rain. Much of the year you don't walk on the lawn so much as splash through it. It's a blessing and a curse.

When it's wet and can't be mowed, plants in the lawn manage not only to grow tall but to blossom, with the result that we can wake up in the morning to see great stretches of the lawn sprinkled with white or yellow or pink or purple. We get impatient with the raggedy look, but Ann never fails to comment on the beauty of those colorful patches. So why think of getting rid of them? Quite outside the question of the cost in time and money of maintaining a large weed-free lawn, do I really want an expanse only of grass, or rather an expanse of only one variety of grass?

With some exceptions, such as thistles, which are a pain, I like the variety of plants in our lawn, and I like the challenge of identifying them all. I don't expect such an interest to be shared by visitors. No one goes to a garden to look at the lawn. No one besides me is going to look down and ask, "What's that little purple thing down there?" It will remain a stretch of green with weeds and wildflowers in it that we walk over to go and look at the peonies and daylilies. But starting three years ago and for the foreseeable future, in addition to being the object of Callander's routine care, it has been and will be the subject of my research.

Maybe it's odd that I started trying to learn the identities of the weeds and wildflowers in our lawn before I had learned the names of the peony varieties, daylily varieties, and hosta varieties we inherited from the previous owners, and I do feel bad that I still don't know them. But in the spirit of plant democracy, I couldn't and can't help feeling that all the plants on our property deserve at least equal scrutiny from their owner, even if they don't necessarily deserve equal care. I should know all the perennials I water and mulch and deadhead, all the evergreens I now have a hard time telling apart, all the ferns and wildflowers in the border between woods and lawn, and all the plants in our lawn.

So my lawn work was looking and learning. What were those wildflowers in it? Some of them I knew because everyone knows them. Individually, dandelions are stunning flowers, and their seedpods equally so, witness the plastic and glass paperweights that display them so ingeniously. Ann enjoys digging dandelions out of the perennial beds with that long thin implement with a V-shaped notch at the end (which one supplier calls an "asparagus knife and weeder"), but she's happy to see them flowering in the lawn, and so am I.

Plantains I knew. Broad-leaved plantains grew very successfully and conspicuously in whole areas of our lawn. One summer Ann suggested we each pull out fifteen a day. We started with the biggest ones, which were the easiest to grasp because their many broad leaves made a good handle for pulling, but their clutch of stubby roots was so strong that several times Ann strained and panted until — oops, over she went backward again with the plant in her hand, like a baseball in a triumphant fielder's mitt. Soon there were bare spots in the lawn wherever those broad leaves had shaded everything else out, with small craters in the center where the roots had been. The piles of pulled plants grew, but while we were eliminating the large plantains, smaller ones were growing large, and fifteen a day wasn't anything like enough. Our lawn still has a lot of them.

There's a broad-leaved plantain in Albrecht Dürer's amazing study of grasses, which in my present state of mind I would pick as my favorite painting of plants — forget the Impressionists or Van Gogh. Dürer's watercolor technique is mind-boggling, but what is so touching is that he should choose such a lowly subject and, what's more, choose to make his dandelions unmistakable without showing them at their attractive best, in full bloom or in seed. He gazed long and intensely at what most of us most of the time wouldn't glance at twice, or even once: dandelions with unopened flowers, a broad-leaved plantain, and a grass and another plant I didn't know until I read Kurt Bluemel's foreword to Rick Darke's *Color Encyclopedia of Ornamental Grasses,* where he identified the one as blue meadowgrass and the other as columbine. Bluemel calls the picture inspiring, and I agree. I can't get enough of it. Late fifteenth century. It's framed above my desk.

Narrow-leaved plantains flourish in our lawn but don't take up as much space as their broad-leaved relatives. When they seed, they take Ann and me back to our childhoods, when we played, she in the south of England and I in the north, competitive games with their seed heads. They are also called English plantains, but I'm sure American kids play with them too. In one game, I hold the stalk of my plantain, as if offering you the seed head. You hit it with your plantain. If you knock my seed head off, you win that round, but if your head flies off, I win. If both heads are left intact, I have a swipe at yours, and so on until there's a winner. If both heads fly off, we start another round with fresh plantains. In the other game, we choose plantains whose stalks are pliable enough to bend double without snapping; we wrap the stalk of our plantain once around itself to form a loop which we pull against the seed head to send it flying off. Whoever shoots his or her head farthest wins. I bet German kids in Dürer's time played those games too.

We try to pull out burdocks with that long tool with the notch. Mercifully, there are very few of them, but their taproots are so deep that the job is almost impossible. Thistles are almost as difficult. But what sort of thistle is this? I don't think any thistle has had time to grow tall enough to flower in our lawn as the much smaller dandelions and plantains have, so I am missing that clue. A leaf shape or some other feature will have to suffice to identify it. Then Ann has another enemy, a weed that spreads at an astonishing rate, undeterred by the thickest mulch, from lawn to perennial bed, where she is forever pulling it out. It's ground ivy. In the lawn it looks fine.

Hugh Johnson, who calls himself an "amateur gardener," says in his superb *Principles of Gardening*, "I have found that a good way to get to know flowers is to pick them and keep them close to me for a few days in a vase." I'm doing that. Ann likes wildflowers in a vase, but she isn't keen to see vases containing nondescript weeds on our kitchen windowsill, and she is even less keen to see them on the dining room table or coffee table, but she tolerates them on my desk, which is my turf.

Hugh Johnson has some typically wise and eloquent pages on weeds. One short passage I try to keep in mind: "Unless you hand-weed your garden you do not know what is in it. Down in the undergrowth with a hand-fork, sorting out the sheep from the goats, you are faced with the task of identifying every plant. I make it a rule not to pull up anything I cannot name. In fact, I name them as I go: a homely catechism of chick-weed, shepherd's purse, groundsel, knotweed (with a few expletives deleted), until suddenly there is a little plant which is none of these." That's admirable advice for when I'm weeding our perennial beds, but also for when I'm examining our lawn. However, it will be a long time before I can say I never "pull up anything I cannot name."

Wildflowers of New York in Color, by William K. Chapman, Valerie A. Chapman, Alan E. Bessette, Arleen Rainis Bessette, and Douglas Pens, with botanical drawings by Philippa Brown, is the book I have been consulting in my lawn wildflower identification program. Plants are arranged in it by color, first of all, then within each color by the physical structure of the flower, then within that subdivision by leaf arrangement. Each plant has a paragraph of pertinent descriptive information, and the color photographs are good.

The best wildflower in the lawn, in my opinion, is creeping thyme. We have several square yards of it as we walk toward the main entrance to the west woods, and the smell as we do so is pure pleasure. When it becomes several square yards of purple in July, it looks good too. It's spreading, and I'm delighted.

White clover proliferates in our lawn, and so does wild strawberry, with a very pretty white flower when you look at it closely. There's plenty of common blue violet, and there is creeping Jenny (shiny round leaves and yellow flower), yarrow, and pussytoes, with fuzzy white flowers and white woolly foliage. Then there is bird's foot trefoil, which, on second thought, has to be my favorite lawn wildflower. It's Ann's favorite. When she sees a bright yellow patch of it, she asks me to tell Callander's not to mow it. Sometimes it covers many square yards, much more than the "leaping tongue of bloom" which was spared by the mower in Robert Frost's "Tuft of Flowers."

I have plenty more wildflowers in our lawn to learn. I like the learning, and I like their presence. I like the idea that they like it here, that I needn't cultivate them; they will just grow. They don't need me.

CHAPTER 9

Flowers of Grass

FOR A WHOLE SUMMER we had a vase of flowers on our dining room table. One week the vase held one type of flower, another week another, and the effect was always interesting and often beautiful. Which was serendipitous, because the flowers hadn't been gathered for their beauty or even to add interest to the table, and they had almost no color to speak of. Ann liked them there anyway. They were grass.

Identifying the grass in our lawn that summer was another phase in the plant identification part of my long-term plan. I had started by trying to identify the wildflowers in the lawn because they stood out here and there, or rather everywhere, in the grass. But what was the grass? During the endless weeks of snow the previous winter, when I yearned to see green again, I had set myself what I thought would be a comparatively easy job for the spring. I thought I should celebrate the lawn's return to view by looking at it closely and learning what grass it consisted of. The lawn was more than a green frame for the perennial beds: it was the second largest visual component of our property, after the woods.

It was what gave the open area its particular character, and it kept its own character despite being continually walked on and continually cut. But while I knew most of the plants in our perennial beds — although after a year of learning I still didn't know those peony, daylily, and hosta varieties — and had made a start on getting to know the wildflowers in the lawn, I had no idea what the lawn's main component was. So when spring and summer proved as miserable in their own way as the preceding winter and the grass shot up during endless weeks of rain, I found myself spending plenty of time indoors comparing grass in a vase with photographs or drawings of grass in books, and I ended up being surprised at how much I liked some of them.

The job of identification was not as easy as I had thought it would be. It wasn't easy, first of all, to really see grass. Yes, it's everywhere, everywhere. But that's the problem. I suspect that I am like many other people, including many other gardeners, whose eyes tend to look not at grass but past it, to plants that are bigger, more interestingly shaped, or more colorful than grass. In a mown lawn, where grass behaves the way we want it to behave, individual plants don't draw attention to themselves because they can't. But even when the lawn does what it wants to do and becomes a meadow, as the one-acre section to the west of our lower lawn does all summer every year because it's so wet that it can't be mowed (and as our whole lawn did one spring, to two feet deep, for the same reason), the plants there look so similar and so unremarkable by comparison with our gardened plants that they still don't stand out, unless in their rather uniform and unprepossessing raggedness. Apart from the weeds and wildflowers, which do draw some attention to themselves, the lawn is all just grass.

But when that spring I did manage to focus on the unmowed lawn, I saw that of course it isn't so much grass and weeds as grasses, in the plural, and scores of other plants, which were weeds if we didn't like them and wildflowers if we did. What I was looking at was the beginnings of what nature does on its own when there is plenty of light and water, and soil of any sort. It was going wild, or natural. It was revealing itself for what it really was. It was fulfilling itself.

Where to start distinguishing between the various grasses? I felt as I assume most birders feel when they try to match up a warbler, particularly in the fall, with one of the warblers in the guidebooks. If even the authoritative authors call them confusing, what hope have I to sort them out? (I don't even try. I only consult a bird book when I know I am likely to find my bird in it, having noted a clearly visible characteristic.) The grasses were like that, to my beginner's eyes: they all looked the same in the lawn and in the books. But when I focused further on the lawn, I saw that many of the grasses were flowering, and some at least of their flowers had obvious differences, and yes, I could spot some of those differences in the books. Among the early flowerers all around me, for instance, were two quite different, very common grasses I had seen all my life but that I couldn't name. Now I can. Roger, who has farmed for decades and knows plenty of grasses and who had flown over from Acaster for another visit, told me immediately what they were: Timothy (*Phleum pratense*) and Orchard Grass (*Dactylis glomerata*), which in England Roger knew as cocksfoot.

Edward Knobel's 1899 *Field Guide to the Grasses, Sedges, and Rushes of the United States* (revised edition, 1977) had excellent drawings of the commonest American grasses on its right-hand pages, where timothy on his Plate 1 and orchard grass on his Plate 7 were instantly recognizable. Timothy's clusters of flowers are packed so densely together at the top of the stem that they look like a smooth thickening of the stem. I can spend a long time looking at this ear, as Knobel calls it, or inflorescence, as other books call it, it's so simple and elegant. Orchard Grass, on the other hand, has one, two, three, or perhaps a few more short side branches which stick out stiffly at the top of its stem, at the ends of each of which are one or two thick clusters of flowers. It's a whole different look and, like so many other grasses, good-looking to my eyes once I had got past its image as nothing to look at because it's nothing but grass.

"Flowers" does seem an odd thing to call those almost colorless things at the top of a grass stem, but that is what they are, although, as in the case of daisies and other "composites," it's not easy for laypeople and amateurs like me to tell precisely which is the flower and which is the collection of flowers. Knobel, who makes the tiny individual flowering unit the final identification key in his *Field Guide,* tries to clarify: "By ear is meant the whole flowering part of a single stem or culm, however complicated and branched. An ear is composed of many small earlets or spikelets, and a spikelet consists of two outer scales, husks or glumes, answering to the calyx of a flower, and containing one, two, or many flowering scales, which enclose the stamens, pistils and fruit; sometimes some flowering scales contain fertile, others sterile flowers." And on the left-hand pages of his book, opposite the very fine drawings, he provides very brief descriptions, about ten to a page (of many more grasses than he illustrates), with hundreds of drawings of these tiny flower units down the margins next to the text.

"Where grasses have a similar appearance," he writes, "the drawing of the spikelet before each name will insure the student finding the right one."

The trouble for me was that a huge number of grasses, despite my looking carefully at them, still had a very similar appearance; the distinguishing features in Knobel's small drawings were themselves not easy to see; and the prospect of examining a flower, or spikelet, under a lens and comparing it to one after another of his drawings was, to say the least, daunting. That's a job for professionals or for serious students of agrostology, itself a term I hadn't known, meaning the study of grasses. (Microsoft Word doesn't know it either.) Knobel used it in the nineteenth century, and it's the title of several college courses available today in this country — as, for instance, at Montana State University, one of whose goals is for students to "develop a personal collection of grasses and grass-like plants of over 120 species." So far I had found two.

I saw that one of the recommended books in that Montana State University course is H. D. Harrington's *How to Identify Grasses and Grasslike Plants,* which was published in 1977, nearly a century after Knobel's book. I thought Harrington would help me out there in the meadow, but I should have opened his book before I bought it, because its title is seriously misleading. No grasses are identified in it. It should have been called something like *A Manual for the Study of Grasses, Including a Complete Visual Glossary of All Technical Terms.* The visual glossary is excellent, but who, other than an agrostologist, knew there were so many technical terms for the often very small parts of a lowly grass?

Nevertheless, my vision was gradually clearing, and I was beginning to see other grasses in our meadow and in the border between lawn and woods that I hoped I could find in Knobel or elsewhere. I was pleased to find that Lauren Brown, in her 1979 book *Grasses. An Identification Guide,* recognizes upfront the difficulties I faced as an amateur. She writes with very little jargon and, like Knobel, provides many drawings of the general appearance of the inflorescences of the commonest plants, concentrating on "their general, shape, color, and texture," that is, what I could see at arm's length with the naked eye.

Lauren Brown's drawings are not as fine as Knobel's, but they are efficient, and it was one of them that got me close to identifying another plant I found and liked in an area I had partially cleared on a slope in the east woods. Roger didn't know it, nor did Leon and Ruth, nor our friend Tom Carty, a professional gardener. In this case it wasn't the top, flowering part that was notable. It was the leaves, blue-green, relatively wide, and interestingly folded over one another in a four- or five-inch mound. I put a whole plant, roots and all, in a saucer on the dining room table, where Ann commented on its interest, thereby letting herself in for a whole summer of different grasses there.

Lauren Brown's drawing made me think our plant must be *Carex laxiflora* (not a grass, it turns out, but a sedge). But then, much later in the summer, I came across a photograph in W. George Schmid's *Encyclopedia of Shade Perennials* of *Carex plantaginea,* which looked just like our plant. And then in Rick Darke's *American Woodland Garden* I saw a color photograph of *Carex platyphylla* which looked even more like our plant. I went on the Web, saw *Carex platyphylla* in drawings and in color photographs on commercial (wholesale and retail) nursery sites and on academic sites, and confirmed that it was the plant growing in our woods. North Creek Nurseries called it blue satin sedge and said it "spreads slowly by rhizomes to form a lovely groundcover. Looking for competition or compliment for Hosta? This is it! An easy to grow and sophisticated new native groundcover choice." Seneca Hill Perennials sold it for six dollars a plant, called it silver sedge, and said, "This must be the most beautiful of our native woodland sedges . . . *C. platyphylla* will adapt to a fairly wide range of soils, tolerating quite dry conditions once established." Those descriptions made me feel good, because that summer I had begun collecting hundreds of these plants from here and there on the slope to form a solid, broad blue-green stripe. I was glad to find that the plant had common names — as far as I could see, many of the other *Carexes* didn't — but then I saw that the Wisconsin State Herbarium, at the University of Wisconsin, called this plant broad-leaf sedge, broad-leaved sedge, broad-leaved wood sedge, and thicket sedge. I decided I should try to remember the Latin name after all. *Carex platyphylla.*

There were two other sedges on our property which were nothing like these *Carexes* but which were equally attractive in their own way. They were very like each other, but the first, dark green bulrush (*Scirpus atrovirens*), flowered in late spring, and the other, umbrella sedge (*Cyperus strigosus*) or nut sedge (*Cyperus esculentus*), flowered in late summer. The dark green bulrush's flower clusters looked like little knobby balls, the umbrella or nut sedge's looked like little toilet brushes, and this plant had long leafy bracts which shoot out sideways from the same place at the top of the stem as the toilet brushes, and it looked good in a vase. But which was it, umbrella or nut? I gathered that it depended on whether it had little hard tubers at the end of its stolons, which meant I was going to have to dig one up and look at its roots, something I couldn't be bothered to do yet. Meanwhile, I read that nut sedge "can be a troublesome weed," so I bet that that was the one in our meadow.

I admit I got mildly hooked that summer by something that is in no way central to most gardeners' preoccupations. I don't plan to develop this interest into a passion or to treat these plants as if they are ornamentals. But I do have a new attitude to our meadow, the one-acre area between the lower lawn and the line of fourteen weeping willows. The meadow is a large part of the lawn, mowed once a year at the most, so it's full of grasses which flower at different times from late spring to late summer. I used to look from the lawn to the willows and into the west woods behind them without glancing at what was between. Now I see bands of differing colors and textures, from the bright green mown lawn in the foreground, through the more muted orchard grass and another grass I have not yet identified whose flowering parts create a light brown haze in the middle distance, to timothy, with its long, slender vertical heads silhouetted against the dark of the woods.

That grass in the middle distance is just one of many that still tantalize me. It has little detectable color on its own, but en masse it's a cloud of pale brown. I have been postponing trying to identify it, which I know will give me a headache, because there are several other grasses very like it on the property, and there are many very like it in Lauren Brown's book. One of them, purple love grass (*Eragrostis spectabilis*), is the only grass in her book she calls "beautiful." It's very like one of ours which isn't in the meadow but hidden away in a tangled border between lawn and woods, an area for which I also have great respect. This plant is one of my favorites, but I will be surprised if it is purple love grass, which Laura Brown says is common in sandy soil, whereas ours is clearly thriving in sodden clay. When I put ours in a vase on our dining room table, Ann commented several times on its beauty.

This plant is typical of the scores of grasses I have been trying to get to know: not a commercial grass like wheat or barley or oats, which I knew already from having seen Roger harvest them at Acaster; not an ornamental grass like those sold at retail garden centers and illustrated in gardening books; but something much more ordinary, a little bit of very successful wildlife, which will keep on growing here without my help unless I actively hinder it by eliminating, for some reason, the meadow and the border between lawn and woods. On the dining room table, it's so self-effacing that you can literally look through it at the person opposite you at dinner, a distinct advantage over many fancy flower arrangements: you don't have to keep moving it, or your head, as you talk. But if you do focus on it, what you see is an extraordinarily delicate and airy structure which is at the same time strong enough to hold its shape without wilting.

Beautiful leaves, beautiful structure of flowering branches, beautiful allover shape — it's odd to think of this as applying to grasses by the side of the road or in an uncared-for tree pit on a city sidewalk, but it's like anything else (almost anything else) in the world: it repays being isolated, framed, or, in our case, put in a vase and looked at. Knobel said in the second sentence of his introduction to his book on grasses: "Aside from their usefulness, their beauty and graceful forms are unsurpassed by any other plants." That may be the hyperbole of a specialist in love with his subject, but I see something now in the grasses and sedges that I didn't before I started my identification program, and aesthetic pleasure is involved. I see it even in such notorious weeds as crab grass (*Digitaria sanguinalis*), with its long, skinny, straight branches full of minute, almost invisible, flowers going off at different angles from the stem, and quackgrass (*Agropyron repens*), with clusters of flowers alternating close to the upright stem. I see it in English rye (*Lolium perenne*), with its wavy stem and clusters of flowers nestled in each concave curve; in manna grass (*Glyceria obtuse*), with many flowers all clustered on small upward-pointing branches to make a thick, dense, oblong shape at the top of the stem; in witchgrass (*panicum capillare*), with a remarkably large explosion of thin branches, each with many distinct spikelets; and in yellow foxtail (*Setaria glauca*), whose head is made up of flowers close to the stem, like timothy's, but drooping in a graceful curve, thick, soft, and furry — asking to be stroked.

Some of these plants get into the perennial beds and flower there along with the plants we traditionally consider more decorative. Here the grasses are weeds, and I pull them out, but not always without a second glance and a second thought. They all look good singly or bunched in a vase. And unlike most other flowers you are used to putting in a vase, you don't have to keep watering them. You don't have to water them at all. They will hold their shape there for just as long as you want to look at them.

CHAPTER 10

A Garden Can Just Happen

I'VE SPENT A LOT OF TIME over the last three years on a slope in the east woods bordering our lower lawn, and somehow a garden — sort of a garden — has materialized there. The fact that the new garden is on a wooded slope and that the garden has appeared with no planning on my part are, I think, connected.

First, the slope. Much of our property slopes, and there have been many times when I wish it didn't. Hauling mulch and compost, for instance, from the piles at the bottom of our property all the way up to our various perennial beds was far more strenuous exercise with the wheelbarrow than I thought I needed before I was finally forced to buy the secondhand golf cart to do the work for me. And I'm continually wondering, shouldn't we have steps up the steep slope at the back of our house to make climbing up to the top of the upper lawn easier? Shouldn't we avoid the risks involved in mowing the steeper parts by planting some other low groundcover there instead of grass? Shouldn't we consider terracing?

On the other hand, slopes are not boring. And they may offer two advantages for a garden that a flat site can't. One is, if there is a flat area below a good viewing place (your house, for instance), you may be able to look down at a garden in its entirety, seeing some or all of the plants at the back as well as those in the middle and the front. And the second is the same but in reverse: you may be able to look up from your house at a garden on an upward slope and see the same thing — the plants at the back (the top) as well as those in the middle and at the front. Flat gardens hide the plants at their back, unless they are tall, until you walk around to see them. I'm not saying that revealing everything is better than withholding something, just that it's impossible on flat sites.

Our house is in the middle of a sloping lawn, so we could, if we wanted to, plant gardens below the house to look down on and above the house to look up at. We haven't done so for two main reasons: one, we enjoy looking across relatively uninterrupted lawn; and two, failures in delivering the desired pictures by a gardener without enough experience and knowledge (me) would be too conspicuous and embarrassing. However, we can see successful examples of the first type of garden on the property of our friends Ruth and Leon, who inspire all gardeners who visit them. The land drops off quite steeply from their house, then levels off until it reaches a stream. What a picture. When you look down from their house, you see a number of large oblong or kidney-shaped gardens surrounded by lawn, most of them a mass of brilliant daylily color in the summer. In the spring, each of them is ringed by innumerable forget-me-nots, so you look down at green pools of bright young daylily foliage sitting in rings of clear bright blue, all surrounded by the green of cut grass. If the site were all flat, you wouldn't see those rings of blue, only the nearest forget-me-nots and daylilies.

As for the second type of garden, I've been working on one in a slightly more inconspicuous and more for-giving area of our property than our upper lawn. You can't see it from the house; it's there on the left as you walk or drive in to the property and on the right when you walk or drive out. It starts at the east edge of the lower lawn and climbs upwards into the shade of par-tially cleared deciduous woods. You can stand on the lower lawn in front of it and see it all, front and back (bottom and top), at one glance. It took a couple of years before I thought of it as a garden, and it is still the slope that should get whatever credit the garden deserves rather than I, who worked there but didn't plan it and didn't really recognize it as a garden until it was almost finished.

Rigorous planning is essential for certain types of garden. Most of the great gardens, probably the best gardens, certainly all formal gardens, were carefully planned. Our friend Debbie Nevins presents plans to her clients that are probably works of art in themselves, complete with three-dimensional models. And Ruth planned colors, dimensions, textures, and times of bloom for at least one of her magnificent perennial beds — mixed shrubs and perennials — on paper, then planted and watched her scheme come gloriously to life. If I were ever to consider attempting perennial beds in the lawn below or above our house, I would plan to plan.

But that's not what happened on our shady east woods slope. What happened was that over the course of three years — well, a garden just happened. I worked there, but there's a very real sense in which I didn't make the garden; the site did. The slope, with its adult iron-woods and white pines, exposed and moss-covered rock ledges, ferns, grasses, sedges, weeds and wildflowers, is the main feature. It's both the frame and the picture within the frame. My plantings, kept subservient to the site (I realize now), have been very slowly improvised rather than deliberately planned. Even the conspicuous shape of this garden, the bottom third of a circle drawn by a curving line of stones as if against the blackboard slope, just happened.

This area, like the west woods, had been an impenetrable tangle of green in the summer, brown in the winter. We had placed an inexpensive wooden bench there to allow us to sit and look across the lower lawn at sunsets. But I wanted to see what was behind the bench and behind the barrier of shrubs in the sloping woods. I clambered through the briars, honeysuckle, and saplings at the edge of the lawn, climbed up to a high flat area, and when I looked down glimpsed a whole new view of the place. It felt good up there. For several weeks I cleared out much of the tangle at the edge, all the saplings, dead trees, and low dead branches, so I could see out more clearly. You could also now see in. The easiest route to the top was a gentle curve between big trees, and I took it every time I went up there. When I recognized that it had become a path (or rather, *the* path), I lined it with stones from a broken-down wall in the woods at the top of the slope. I put a white cast-iron chair and a white cast-iron table up at the top as a sort of signal that there was something worth climbing to: a place to sit with a cup of coffee in the early morning and watch the steam rising from the lawn below or, if there were no mosquitoes, a place to come with a glass of wine in the evening and watch the sun sink behind the west woods on the other side of the lawn. The first time I coaxed Ann up there (in the middle of the day), she was surprised at the new view. She too liked the place.

The first plants I brought to the area were hundreds of forget-me-nots generously given by Ruth and Leon, who knew how much I admired their extraordinary rings of clear sky blue. I put them at the edge of the lawn where the tangle of brush had been, down at the bottom of the slope. That started a summer-long process of moving plants into the area behind them. They were all common as dirt, they were all low, and they were all notoriously aggressive spreaders and so potentially invasive, all immediately available, some of them much too available where they were. Not the sort of plants you show off with pride, but just right to cover this large area and keep it moderately weed-free. (Famous last thoughts.)

I pulled out ajuga from our lawns, where it had become established, where it was not particularly welcome, and where mowing would probably never give it a chance to flower anyway. I moved hundreds of these little plants to form a big patch at the lowest part of the site, right at the edge of the lawn next to the forget-me-nots. Several hours of afternoon sun ignited a blaze of deep blue in the spring and kept its crinkled leaves a purplish brown the rest of the year. I moved clumps of periwinkle from beside the road outside our property to behind the ajuga. Its pale blue flowers are a bonus in the spring, but its dark green foliage was the point. Behind the periwinkle, I moved many light, shiny green pachysandra plants, and behind the pachysandra another band of dark green vinca. Then, up at the top of the slope, just below the seat and table, the notoriously invasive goutweed or bishop's weed (*Aegopodium podagraria*), whose cream and pale green variegated leaves would be visible even at a distance. Finally, I couldn't resist buying a couple of hundred grape hyacinths (*Mus-*

cari armeniacum), whose flowers, a different bright blue again from the blues of forget-me-not, ajuga, and periwinkle, had lit up another area of our property so brilliantly in the spring.

I found that I was planting blocks of what would be different blues in the spring and contrasting greens at all other times. It was the first of two artificial features in what would otherwise have remained a bit of pleasant weedy and wildflower woodland. But I still wasn't thinking of the area as a garden, I was merely seeing how groundcovers by the side of the road or overrunning our gardens elsewhere could replace the weeds that had rushed in as soon as more light had become available, and I thought I might as well line them up or block them off so they would be noticeable from a distance.

I did some more thinning out and filling in. In his third visit to us from Acaster, Roger helped me take down five trees, two of them riddled with ants, hollowed out by pileated woodpeckers, dying, and threatening to fall on the utility lines they were hanging over. When they were gone, the view in and out was clearer, although as you looked at the area from the lawn, it still didn't look like much of anything.

I was spreading the plants leftward without knowing when or where I was going to stop. But then I found that as I worked on the left, I was treading a new path up to the top, so why not make it official by lining it with stones from the broken-down wall, as I had lined the one on the right? When I had finished, the stones lining the two paths, one to the right and the other to the left, met at the bottom and described a large curve, the bottom third of a circle, quite visible from the lawn. This second artificial feature effectively distinguished the whole area as, well, something.

I brought Ann to the lower lawn, pointed to the slope, and said, "Is there something there?" I was thinking of the feature on David Letterman's *Late Show* on television in which he and Paul Shaffer decide whether some bizarre act or thing amounts to Anything or not. After a growing chorus of "Is this *Anything*?" a curtain is raised to reveal Whatever-It-Is flanked on one side by a beautiful woman twirling hoops round her scantily clad body and on the other by a beautiful woman grinding sparks from something on her scantily clad middle with what looks like a chain saw. There was no razzmatazz where I was pointing, and Dave and Paul would have smiled, shaken their heads, and said, No, sorry, that was Nothing At All, but in our quieter context Ann was obliging and said yes, it did seem to be Something.

Was it a garden? What defines a garden? A clear edge would seem to be an important element, defining it literally. This area on the slope was still pretty messy, but that curve of stones and the different bands of color within it definitely distinguished it from the areas to its right and left. The curve told me where I should now be concentrating my work, and that having started a somewhat geometrical arrangement, I might as well carry on with it, carry it through. Now I needn't bother with the area to the left of the new path. It could grow as weedy as it wanted: the greater the contrast, the better. I started to fill up spaces in the segment with other plants that were already growing on the slope or on a similar slope in a different area of woods. I started to garden.

I moved Christmas ferns and maidenhair ferns into two rectangular blocks, and another common fern whose name I have not yet learned into two separate horizontal strips and two lines inside the stone curve, to define it even more strongly. There were a lot of *Carex platy-*

phylla, the beautiful blue-green sedge I was proud of identifying in books and on the Web, all over the slope, so I moved them too into three horizontal streaks. There were Jack-in-the-pulpit (*Arisaema*) plants throughout the woods: two more blocks for the slope. And a white sage with silver gray foliage (*Artemisia ludoviciana*) was running all over a perennial bed: another block.

I had in mind a tapestry of blocks of differing groundcovers, a sort of groundcover quilt, but a year changed my mind. The next spring and summer were so wet that I never had to water my transplants, a great convenience among all the annoyances of the weather, but the weeds went crazy. With constant rain and with more sunlight pouring onto it than it had had for years, suddenly the slope was blanketed with weeds, laying the wrong sort of mosaic all over my geometry, and I have never spent so much time pulling and digging them out. Garlic mustard pulls up fairly easily, but it is so prolific that it appears to find and fill every available square inch of space.

The ajuga flowered wonderfully, but weeding it became impossible, and it gradually disappeared under grass. Most people try to get bugle out of their lawn. I had to get lawn out of our bugle, which didn't seem fair. And I wasn't pleased when Ann asked me in the evening what I had been doing all day and all I could say was, "Weeding the slope." "Weeding the woods!" She thought I was nuts. "Seems a weird type of gardening, doesn't it?" Yes, but now that I had committed so many hours to that slope, I didn't want weeds to take it over. Ground ivy was her enemy in our perennial beds, garlic mustard on that slope was mine. (Although I read that it's good to eat in salads.)

After days of weeding, I stood on the lawn and looked

at the area. Not satisfactory. Messy and scrappy. I thought, Keep It Simple, Stupid. I embarked on a radical simplification program. Move all the ferns into one long horizontal line, ditto the artemisia, the sedge, the vinca, and the pachysandra. Then, when weeds came up, which they would surely continue to do, at least we should be able to make out vague horizontal stripes of different colors. They were the commonest plants, but in an unusual arrangement.

We'll see how it turns out in the coming years. I realized when I looked at all those weeds that I had been guilty of exactly the laziness that Hugh Johnson had warned me against in a section on groundcovers in *Principles of Gardening*. "Groundcover can maintain order, but it cannot impose it," he writes. "It is no use hoping that by planting ivy [in my case, pachysandra] or periwinkle — however densely and lavishly — in ground infested with serious permanent weeds you will eventually smother them into submission." That's what I had hoped would happen on my slope. "There is nothing labor-saving about groundcover in the early stages. Quite the contrary," he goes on. "Because you are giving your planting a long lease on the ground in question it needs unencumbered possession." Instead of just swinging away with my mattock to expose soil and putting plants in it, I should also have dug out or poisoned all visible weeds, then watched the bare soil for three summer months before planting. I should have lavished just as much care on the slope as on any new bed of flowering perennials with crisp edges.

But I hadn't started to think of the slope as a garden until it was too late. I hadn't planned. And the truth is, I'm ambivalent about how much I want it to look and behave like a well-groomed garden. On the one hand, I want the slope to look "natural." On the other hand, those stripes and that curve of stones make it clearly very artificial. I can't have it both ways. If it's going to look natural, it will inevitably have weeds. I don't want weeds, so I have to face it: I've let myself in for a lot of weeding for a long time.

I put two more white cast-iron chairs at the top of the new garden so three people could sit there. But what surrounded the seats and table was a rather unprepossessing collection of briars, white snakeroot, and garlic mustard. I weedwhacked the area and it looked better. Then I raided a pile of tree trunks I had put nearby when I cleared the area and laid them at the feet of the living trees to make a circle, not unlike the circle in the west woods where Em got married. I sprayed RoundUp on everything within the circle, and suddenly it looked good and felt interesting to sit in and look down at the lawn and at the vague stripes of groundcovers.

So the slope is changing. I'll get those stripes less vague, more defined, more of a contrast to what is on either side of them, and more of a contrast to what it was, more of a garden. It's one of several places I regret not having photographed before I worked on it. I hadn't photographed the slope in its state when we bought the property because it wasn't distinctive. It was trees, shrubs, and weeds: a lot of solid green, undistinguished like a lawn or a meadow is undistinguished until, for whatever reason, you happen to look at it closely. And I hadn't photographed it because I hadn't known at the time that something quite different would materialize there. I would like to show people, and remind myself, what it used to look like, but all I have now is my memory of the way it was, and my memory is becoming more and more like the way it was, indistinct.

CREATURES

CHAPTER 11

Keeping Them Out

IT WAS AN EARLY Sunday morning in June a few years ago when I saw the fawn in the grass ten yards from our front door. It must have been born a few hours before. I walked around it, went back for the camera, came out again, and photographed it. It lay there quite still, although I could see it was breathing. I went back inside, woke Ann, and told her she had to get up, put on shoes, and come outside, to which her response was an outraged "You have to be kidding," and when I persisted, "This had better be good."

She followed me outside in her nightdress and shoes (we worry about deer ticks) and let out a series of whispered exclamations and motherly cries of endearment when she saw what was still lying there absolutely still. We spent several minutes debating in whispers. We do not like deer on our property. Not at all. Full-grown deer are very beautiful creatures, but many of the plants I like to look at they like to eat, and this little thing was going to become a full-grown deer, thinking of our property as home. Knock it on the head? I couldn't do that, and Ann certainly wouldn't let me. Phone Roberta, who loves all animals and knows so much about them, for advice? What local authority would help?

The fawn didn't move. It was amazingly beautiful. We felt silly standing over it whispering, so we started talking. Then we saw the fawn's eyes move, its ears pick up, then its head. Then it lifted its body onto four very unsteady legs and wobbled off to the woods at the bottom of our lawn. Almost every day for the rest of that year we saw a fawn jumping around its mother everywhere on our property, suckling while she browsed until Ann or I chased them both off. The fawn is almost certainly one of the three or four full-grown deer — sometimes it's six or seven — that now patrol our property every day. I made my photograph of it as a baby into the Windows wallpaper for my desktop, so it appears whenever I turn on my computer. I live with it inside and outside.

It was about the time of that fawn's appearance that I started to think seriously about what to do about these animals. I had pulled I don't know how many deer ticks from my skin. I hadn't had Lyme disease, but friends had. Our car hadn't hit any of the countless deer browsing right next to the speeding traffic on the Taconic, but friends had hit them and wrecked their cars, surviving themselves only with great luck. But as a gardener, I was getting disheartened. The deer wanted to eat the plants I wanted to grow, and it was becoming more and more of a problem. We called every deer we saw Doreen, as we had called every dog we saw thirty years ago Fred. (Some things don't change.) Doreen was our Enemy, and still is.

A well-aimed bullet would be the quickest solution, and I love venison, but Ann won't let me consider it. "You're not going to buy a gun, are you? I don't want guns around here. Are you going to become a member of the National Rifle Association? Next, you'll tell me you're going to vote Republican." Well, I wasn't thinking of that, no, but I was thinking of letting the man who services our boiler hunt our deer. He's licensed, and he offered to shoot them and give us venison. "No," Ann says whenever I remind her that I kept his phone number. "We can't have people firing guns within range of our neighbors' houses."

Even if I were able finally to convince Ann that our neighbors and their houses would not be at risk, I couldn't get over her final argument: "How could you do that to one of those beautiful things?" Our problem is not just legal, political, and ethical, it's aesthetic and personal, and I see her point. We saw one of those deer take its first wobbly steps. We saw it gradually losing the dappled patterning on its skin, gradually becoming the elegant thing it now is. I would find it difficult to see it die on our property or have it killed here.

Getting to know our groundhog family complicated our feelings about those animals too. I hate what they do to our plants — once they chomped twenty newly bought violas down to the soil in one night — but who can resist the sight of a parent groundhog being followed around on the lawn by two baby groundhogs, one of which keeps climbing on its back for a free ride? Come to think of it, when we saw Graham the groundhog sitting bolt upright, forepaws up at its chest, staring at us with one of our potentilla flowers sticking out of its mouth, didn't we have to smile even as we were jumping up and down with rage? Killing things you have called cute gets to be difficult.

One morning, very early, I saw two fawns leave the sides of two older deer, race each other across the hundred and seventy-five yards at the bottom of our lawn, turn around, and race back. I imagined them reporting the result of the race to their parents, who kept on eating grass. Then suddenly they were off again, racing all the way across and back, and I wondered which one won that time. Had they each won a race, or is one of them up two to nothing? Asking myself questions like that, I know yet again that I'm not going to be able to persuade myself, let alone Ann, that they should die. And anyway, even if I could, wouldn't we still have a problem? Wouldn't other deer, attracted by the same succulent plants that the dead ones liked, come along to fill their place? More and more killing.

But it's not just our problem. There's an overpopulation of these creatures, and controlled culling has been endorsed by no less an authority than the leading editorial writer of the *New York Times*. Our qualms would certainly strike any livestock farmer as the height of silly sentimentalism. Ann's uncles, who were not farmers but miners in the north of England, always kept a pig in their backyard to eat the next year. During the year in which they were fattening it up, it became part of their family; they gave it a name and played with it until the moment they had to kill it. Every part of its body was used for every type of delicious dish. They wouldn't want to hear our doubts about killing a pest for its good meat; hunters would simply not understand us, nor would most farmers.

If I couldn't kill those deer, maybe I could give them just enough of a jolt with a BB gun or a catapult to make them wary of approaching our perennials? Most people I mentioned this idea to thought it would waste my time and have no effect, and Roberta, who kisses every animal she can get close to, worried that I would hit Doreen in the eye. I thought that if I aimed at its butt I would definitely miss its eye, so I didn't rule out the idea.

Or we could keep them out with a big fence. The trouble was, a fence has to be high and long. I saw a deer jump over the snow banked at the side of our dirt road, clearing six feet with no problem. And I didn't want what the previous owners of our property had: those three electrified wires strung from insulator to insulator on tree trunks at the border between lawn and woods all round, a sort of inner perimeter and an ugly barrier to our walking in the woods. I would want to install a *fence* fence, a high one deep in the woods at the outer perimeter of our property, but that was far too expensive a proposition.

So it was back to spraying our hostas, lilies, daylilies, and filipendula with a variety of unpleasant liquids. At one impressive garden on a garden tour last year, I asked the owner and designer how they kept the deer, which we could all see in a nearby field, away from their colorful perennials. They said they threw a mixture of egg, pepper, and garlic on them, so I got the ingredients, put the mixture in a big bucket, let it sit for a few days, and threw it on the plants. That evening Ann said, "What's that disgusting smell around the phlox?" I had to confess that when I applied that mixture I myself had almost thrown up.

Then a neighbor who sells perennials told me that deer used to sweep through her garden every night, eating whatever they could, until the night they came up against her new solar-powered two-strand electric fence. She heard *"pfft!"* sounds all night long, and they never came through again: they came past on either side of her garden, but they left her perennials alone. She swore by this system: two strands strung on small posts, with reflective foil every few yards which she coated with peanut butter to attract them. One sniff or taste and, zap, they were gone.

So I made my way round the perimeter of our property and figured that yes, maybe I could install one of those. I measured the yardage, and a helpful salesperson at an agricultural supply store calculated how many corner posts I would need, how many smaller posts, how many yards of wire, how many insulators. I calculated how many tags to attach to the wire to attract the deer and how much peanut butter to spread on the tags to zap them.

I got excited. No more hoof marks in the damp soil ever again. No more deer droppings on the lawn. No more looking down at gnawed-off stumps of perennials and telling Ann, "Sorry, no flowers this year from that one." No more being woken in the morning by Ann flying out of our bed and charging up our back lawn in her nightgown, cursing at Doreen. No more driving back into our property after a movie to see bright eyes staring back at our headlights. A few zaps from our fence and they would be our neighbors' problem, not ours.

I started clearing a path for the fence. I took hand saw, chain saw, loppers, and weedkiller into the woods. The path had to be so many feet wide so Doreen could see the reflecting tags. It would have to go straight here, then turn a corner up there and go as straight as possible, to limit the number of corner posts that would be needed. Saw, lop, check on direction, saw, lop, take a rest, saw, spray, lop — day after day. Was this going to work? How easy would it be to bang in posts among these rocks? To string the wires tight up and down these slopes? I was going to have to keep this path permanently clear, to prevent growing plants and falling branches from breaking the circuit. Might I also have to keep peanut-buttering the tags? And what about the entrance to our property? Did I want to keep wires linked across the entrance that we and other people would have to unlink every time we drove in? If we didn't, wouldn't deer simply walk in up the drive, then play havoc when they couldn't get out again, not being bright enough to realize that their only exit was the entrance? I remembered that when I was researching these fences on the Web, their manufacturers regularly described their product with a word that now suddenly seemed ominous — "temporary."

The day I finished the path, I told Ann that I had decided not to install and maintain a fence. It was definitely a moment for a derisive comment, but amazingly she refrained. I think she was as relieved as I was at the thought that I would not be doing all that. A few weeks later, Lucy stayed with us for a weekend and congratulated me on having created an excellent new path around Ginger.

So I'm back to having Callander's stake and net our best shrubs and small trees in the winter and I spray gross stuff on them the rest of the year, not a very satisfactory defense. What else can we do? Grow only so-called deer-resistant plants? It's a good idea. Ann and I love our alliums, catnip, lavender, and Russian sage, and I do plan to grow more of them. But we love our daylilies, and I love lilies. Leon and Ruth have thousands of daylilies, and I admire their philosophical attitude to these problems almost as much as their magnificent garden. When Ann and I first asked them about deer, they said they were simply resigned to losing twenty percent of their flowers every year. Then they bought Jules and Jim, two big, bouncy black dogs, who keep deer away and who destroy only about the same percentage of their flowers as the deer had.

In the absence of an impossibly expensive barricade around our property, and while netting is only so-so effective, and the perfect spray hasn't been invented and perhaps never will be, and without a determined program of killing, I don't see much alternative to our adopting Leon and Ruth's philosophical attitude if we plan to continue growing plants Doreen likes to eat. But being philosophical isn't easy — I suppose, by definition. In the winter, hoofprints in the snow, droppings, and bright urination stains make it impossible not to see precisely where Doreen likes to walk on our property. She really appreciates my new path.

CHAPTER 12

Indoors and Outdoors

ANN AND I ARE SITTING at the breakfast table, reading separate parts of the same newspaper. One of us is absorbing the regional news, the other the international news. It's quiet. The coffee is good.

"James, there's a fly in the room."

I can hear it buzzing around. Then there's quiet again, then more buzzing.

"James?"

"Mm?"

"There's a fly in the room."

"Yeah. It's over there by the window."

Silence, then buzzing again. Ann gets up, searches for the fly swatter, locates it, and smashes up and down the window. She comes back to the table and sits down. "Got it," she says, and we settle back to reading. But I know it won't be long before there's a question.

"Where do they come from?" she asks, with a mixture of exasperation and genuine astonishment. "Can you believe it? How do all these flies get in?"

Ann is a city girl and proud of it: one fly in the house is one too many, and if we see more than a couple in a week, they are "all these flies." I'm the country boy, the gardener, the family authority on wildlife, and I should know the answer to her question, but I don't. I don't know whether the fly snuck in when we opened a door or a window, which we do as briefly and as seldom as possible, or whether it made its way down the chimney into the house, or whether it started life as an egg laid in the house some time ago and has just now become an adult; if the latter, I don't know when and how its parents got in. I have to admit, though, that finding out the answer isn't a priority for me. At Hutton-le-Hole there was no wondering about such things. We left our doors and windows wide open in fly weather. There were no screens. We hung a strip of flypaper in the kitchen, replacing it when its orange glue was black with dying flies. We inspected cold cooked meat very carefully for maggots before carving, and occasionally found some. Looking back, I am amazed that I don't remember Aunt B being distraught about rats in the walls, mouse nests in our clothes closets, or maggots on the meat we were about to eat.

Maggots. Taboo words don't faze Ann, but "maggots" comes close. I think her family in London had refrigerators much earlier than we did at Hutton, so she never saw maggots in her house. If she were ever to ask at our breakfast table, "Where do all these maggots come from?" I guarantee she would be near hysteria unless or until the occurrence was so regular that she was used to it, which is unthinkable. Anyway, before that could happen, I would most certainly make finding the answer to the question a priority. I don't like maggots at all either.

Animals are usually cuter to human eyes when they are immature. Kittens, puppies, baby chimps, and those baby groundhogs and fawns we see out there every year at Ginger: they're all more adorable than their parents. But the rule doesn't apply to maggots, which are immature flies but which are way higher up the grossness scale. Is that because of their slimy, squirmy, legless look? Or because they are more unpleasant to squash, so we have to carry them outside to dispose of them? (Where they can perform the useful function in a garden of breaking down rotten material and returning nutrients to the soil.) Or because we connect them with putrefying flesh? (Come to think of it, eggs laid in our house would become maggots before they became flies, and I'm sure we don't have the sort of food that maggots like to eat readily available for them, so that fly must have flown in.) Whatever the reason, I don't mind flies, but maggots I mind.

How you react to such things is, I think, largely a matter of how used you are to them. I can imagine circumstances in which I would get used to seeing and even handling a lot of maggots: at Acaster, my father's gardener used to hang dead squirrels from the branch of a tree and put a bucket under them to catch all the maggots falling from the carcass. The more that fell into the bucket, the more good bait for his next fishing trip. In some parts of the world, I have read, people eat maggots, not cooked but live and squirming. I suppose if I were hungry enough, I could do that, but right now it's hard to imagine. And Ann would, I am sure, prefer to die of starvation.

Spiders vary on the grossness-scariness scale, according to size and species. When I hear "James, there's a spider in the shower," I know that that isn't just a descriptive statement. It's a request or a command, depending on the nature of the beast and on whether Ann is clothed or naked. If it has a small body and long legs,

Ann is impressed when I pick it up in my fingers. If it's fat and hairy and moving quickly, she is still fairly impressed when I remove it, but I have to do it with a piece of paper and a glass jar. I wouldn't mind putting the skinny one somewhere else in the house so it can eat intrusive flies and mosquitoes, but Ann prefers it to be outside, and the fat hairy one I make very sure goes outside, because otherwise, as Ann points out and I have to agree, if it wanders around anymore inside, we might feel it walking over our faces in bed in the middle of the night.

Ann and I don't differ greatly in our attitude toward animals, particularly when they are gross or scary or annoying, but we differ just enough to make me wonder occasionally whether the difference is gender-related. On the whole, I think it's more a matter of what each of us has got used to. If I had been a London lad and she a Yorkshire country lass, I might have become the squeamish one and she the nonchalant. No, it's not that I'm a tough male and she's a frail female, although it does seem that mosquitoes find her soft, pleasant-smelling skin more tempting than mine, a fact which really, well, bugs her. If mosquitoes are around, they go for her far more than they go for me, and they raise much bigger bumps on her skin than on mine, bumps which itch and get scratched and linger for weeks. Her complaint that it's unfair sounds like an accusation.

Luckily, mosquitoes aren't around Ginger much at all. Ann gets attacked offsite. Despite being surrounded by woods, we never see or hear mosquitoes in our house (famous last words) and amazingly few on our decks when we sit there in the evening having a drink. We never thought to ask the previous owners about mosquitoes when we were buying the property, but it now strikes us as crucial information all home buyers should make sure they possess. Lack of mosquitoes adds to the value of a property. For people like Ann, mosquitoes make the difference between wanting to go outside and going outside.

As far as Ann is concerned, the outdoors is wonderful, but it should stay outdoors. The house should keep out the rain and wind and cold and all living things except our two jade plants and our two selves. I tend to view visits by insects and spiders and the occasional ant as natural, even routine, occurrences rather than crises, but I don't mind getting them out promptly and keeping them out as efficiently as I can.

Ann's view of the relationship between indoors and outdoors changes slightly when we go out onto the decks, which are good places to eat breakfast on a warm morning, have lunch under the umbrella in the middle of the day, or drink in the evening. Then she views the decks as more indoors than outdoors: she thinks that we should be the only living things there while we eat and drink. There are no mosquitoes, but sometimes we are visited by slow-moving hornets or fast-moving wasps. When I was a kid at Hutton, we often had afternoon tea in the garden and picnic lunches on the moors, and whenever we did, wasps showed up as soon as we unwrapped our sandwiches and unscrewed the Thermos flask of tea. Aunt B told us that it was our food, not us, that the wasps were interested in, so we waited till they landed on our plates, then we squashed them with our plastic knives and carried on eating. In contrast, absolutely nothing in my experience makes Ann move so dramatically as a wasp. If a wasp approaches her, she is on her feet, ducking and weaving and thrashing about, running one way, then back again, flailing all the time, and yelling "James, James!" in exasperation. When I suggest she cool it, she gets angrier, her actions goad the wasp into wild flight motions, they both become more and more frantic until Ann dashes into the house with her food, cursing and slamming the screen door shut.

In the evening, as we sit with a drink on the back deck, we like to watch the bat fly around scooping out of the air little insects which otherwise might be annoying us. It sleeps during the day in the closed-up umbrella in the middle of the table, coming out at dusk for food. It has been "the bat" (actually Benny the bat) for a few years because we haven't seen more than one at a time, and we hope that is because there aren't enough mosquitoes to keep more than one well fed. I put a bathouse high on the side of our house, so we wouldn't have to keep sweeping its droppings from our table, but so far it hasn't been tempted. At lunchtime, Ann won't leave the house until I have opened up the umbrella and let Benny fly sleepily off. One time it flew straight to the screen door behind which Ann was recoiling, and it hung there until I nudged it off so she could come out, sighing and rolling her eyes.

Windows, screens, and screen doors are wonderful things. We have a lot of them, and we have spent many cumulative hours looking through them at birds and animals larger than insects and spiders from our animal-free rooms. From our bedroom, from the breakfast table, from the kitchen sink, from the living room, from Ann's desk, and from our bathroom we watch hummingbirds whirring from flower to flower, red-tailed hawks being mobbed by blue jays, chickadees and nuthatches at the feeder, swallows swooping nearer and nearer to the bluebird house on the upper lawn until finally, when they are within inches of its entrance, they are pounced on by its owner, a bluebird that has been watching them as attentively as we have.

Every spring a male cardinal mistakes his reflection in our windows for a rival and flies at it. He starts early in the morning, and his repeated banging earns curses from Ann, for whom any animal noise that wakes her is as inconsiderate as a garbage truck. The banging continues throughout the day for weeks, raising questions about the solidity of our glass, the abundance of the beautiful bird's testosterone, and the smallness of its brain.

But the cardinal's banging at the window, so different from its wonderfully penetrating whistling, the loudest song we hear all year, is nothing compared to what a yellow-bellied sapsucker had in store for us last year. This male practiced its drum burst on various hollow objects on our property — it tried an empty birdhouse, then the metal covering for our propane gas tank — before finally settling on the aluminum gutter at the corner of our bedroom at the back of the house. He started hammering at five-fifteen in the morning, much earlier than any garbage trucks in our experience and much louder, because he was only a few feet from our heads. Ann was beside herself. "Yellow-bellied sapsucker" quickly joined "Scum-sucking pig" (quoting Brando in *One-Eyed Jacks*) as a favorite term of abuse. Every twenty minutes or so the bird banged away until I put netting over the gutter and it moved to the gutter at the corner of the living room. This was the other side of the house and far enough away for us to be able to sleep through the noise, and the bird could not have found a better spot for its purposes. The long, reverberating gutter above the front deck amplified and broadcast its sapsucker macho message down over the lower lawn and all around. Its rhythm stuck in my head and sounded familiar. I finally decided it was almost exactly the rhythm of the opening burst of Beethoven's eleventh String Quartet in F minor, opus 95, although its notes were all the same pitch, and there was no variation whatsoever. The bird kept it up day after day and Ann began to find it endearing, at least after she had had breakfast and was wide awake. She walked right up to it and talked to it. I got close to it too while it was performing, but as soon as I raised the camera and tried to focus, it flew off. One day Ann happened to be asking it whether it hadn't found a cute lady sapsucker yet when she noticed just such a bird looking up at it and listening to its banging "admiringly," as she described it. As she chatted to them both, they flew off, and we never heard a bang, not even a tap, on the gutter again. The courtship, we concluded, had been a resounding success.

We have very pleasant views from our windows: spacious lawn, perennial beds, shrubs, trees. As the gardener, I tend to look out at the plants and like to think that the perennial beds are the main points of attraction on our property. But I can't look for long without seeing movement on the ground out there. Most of the four-legged animals are bigger and slower than the birds, and they are much quieter, but they are every bit as entertaining and annoying as we watch from inside. Where did they come from? What are they going to do next? Chipmunks are cute whatever they are doing, and squirrels are fine until they take over the bird feeder, and rabbits, groundhogs, and deer are fine until they get near the perennial beds. "Ann, look what's on the back lawn," I say, and she comes immediately and gets very excited — delighted when there are babies with their parents, indignant at what the adults get up to. She nearly always ends up dashing out, gesticulating, yelling, and giving chase. It's a great last act of the show, and there will be many more performances.

In the best weather Ann is outside much of the day. She finds skimming the swimming pool a calming experience and does it daily, enlisting my help and sympathy when there are things larger than leaves floating in it. ("James, there's an animal in the pool.") She takes a dip in the freshly skimmed pool herself, she weeds, she walks around, and she reads in the sun. She loves reading outside on warm sunny days, but if an insect bothers her, she is back indoors in a flash. As a productive and successful writer, she is happy to return to her computer inside. I'm outside whatever the weather, most of the day.

What keeps me out there? It's not just what I am doing to the plants, trying to make them look better and trying to make the whole place look better. It's being in nature. That's the word that best describes it. Ann says she agrees with Woody Allen's line "I am two with Nature," but I like feeling that I'm part of it, in it. Gardening isn't only watching over the plants as they grow upward and outward so slowly that I can't see the process but have to keep checking to see how many inches a week they have moved. It's noticing the small mammals which vanished when they saw or heard me coming outdoors but which will reappear if I'm not too noisy or move too suddenly. It's being close to all these things I see moving around me as I work among the plants. We are told that the healthier our plants are, the better able they are to resist disease, so I try to grow healthy plants, but surely too the healthier our plants are, the more they are appreciated by the creatures whose legs and wings and mouth parts are adapted to crawl and fly among them and chew them and sip from them and haul bits of them from place to place. At any rate, just as it is movement that grabs our attention when we are looking out at the perennial beds from inside, so here it is movement at much closer range that keeps distracting me as I bend over pruning or kneel weeding.

Gardens are dynamic environments, complete with an extraordinary collection of animals at every level on the cuteness, grossness, scariness, and annoyance scales. I love to see as many worms as possible, because I know they are helping to enrich and aerate our soil, and I don't mind handling them. Ann would never handle a worm. What I'm not crazy about handling is slugs, which I think are as gross as maggots, and I don't like squashing them. Japanese beetles I can squash with my fingers, which revolts Ann but seems to be the best way to kill them quickly when I don't have a bucket handy with soapy water to flick them into. Other beetles I like, ladybugs for instance, which are good-looking and eat plant-eating bugs. I hate the look of a tick, especially when the front part of its body is burrowed into my skin and the rest of it is filling up with my blood. I take being bitten or stung almost for granted, like being scratched by prickles or thorns, but I worry about becoming allergic to insect stings, and I worry that that tick may be carrying Lyme disease. New York's Columbia County is the tick capital of the world, but at least I needn't worry about scorpions or poisonous snakes or tarantulas.

Then there are the bees, butterflies, and birds, which don't fly far away when I come out of the house. I can't have enough of the sound of bees and the sight of butterflies around the lavender. As for birds, I would find our garden without birds on the lawn or singing in the trees a sadder, an infinitely sadder, place than it is. A garden can look wonderful in a good color photograph or seen from inside the house through a window, but it's not like being in the garden, with the feel of the sun or wind, the sight of insects on the flowers and leaves, the smell of earth and flowers, and the sound of birds all around.

Not all birds sound beautiful. Nuthatches wheeze, blue jays shriek, and the even louder squawks of the four crows on our lawn could never be called endearing. "Can you believe that racket?" Ann asks every morning as she wakes to their noise. (There are a lot of things about the country, animals particularly, Ann still can't believe. If by chance she sees more than four big birds in a tree, she is apt to say "Oh my God, Alfred Hitchcock!")

It's true that crow squawks have none of the charm of a chickadee's song, or a tufted titmouse's, or a robin's, or a thrush's, or a cardinal's, but there is one time of the day at one time of the year when the squawks play their part perfectly in a glorious all-out chorus. One of the best experiences in my year is waking up before dawn in the spring, going outside in the silence, listening to the first bird in the dark, then hearing more and more birds join in as a glimmer of light appears in the west, then being surrounded by a truly prodigious volume of sound. They keep it up as the outlines of trees and shrubs become clearer, then gradually quieten until by the time I can distinguish colors they are done for the day.

I will hear each of the birds singing or squawking or clucking solo throughout the day, but I won't hear that full-blast chorus again till the next day's dawn. Having the full experience means setting an alarm, something which Ann views as even more outrageous than crows, cardinals, yellow-bellied sapsuckers, or garbage trucks waking her in what she calls the middle of the night. So I leave the window next to my side of the bed wide open (screen in place, of course) in the hope that, hours before she stirs, I may wake to that truly unbelievable racket again. And that's how many of my days do start at that time of the year. It's too early to start on the list of jobs I compiled for myself the day before, but there's no better way to start thinking about which I will tackle first.

CHAPTER 13

Outside the Windows

WHEN ANN WORKS, she likes to have as many consecutive hours to herself in her study as possible before hunger late in the morning or the need for a drink late in the afternoon intrudes on her consciousness. I am not encouraged to interrupt. However, there are not many mornings or afternoons in which I don't suddenly hear a loud whisper: "James, come here!" She wants me to come and look, not at an extraordinary error in one of her competitors' textbooks, but at the furry oblong object browsing in the lower lawn, then sitting suddenly upright like a portly Dickens gent staring at us with a full mouth. The corner windows of her study are small and close to the east woods, and the view from them is somewhat obscured by a very healthy Rose of Sharon, but a groundhog can still catch her eye, and she seldom ignores it. I'm summoned to admire it even if I happen to be working inside myself.

As it happens, I don't mind my work in the living room being interrupted by Ann or by any animal and bird activity outside the windows. And there's plenty of it. Ann wouldn't get much work done here. Ahead of me and slightly to the left are the French doors and windows on either side of them, giving me a good view of the front deck, which is a stage for animal performance — typically chipmunks chasing each other from one end to the other, or robins hopping and listening, apparently under the impression that it's a lawn of a different color and texture from the real lawn a few yards away, or chickadees and bluejays stopping at the deck railings to peck at something or just to perch and look nervously around. Most of the time I prefer looking out of the window to looking at my computer screen, but it has to be something exceptional for me to urge Ann to drop her work for a minute and come and look.

The big attraction, or distraction, outside the living room last spring was on my right, where the front deck is covered to create a porch for the front door. That's where I can take off filthy clothes in the summer or stamp off snow in the winter before entering the house. The evening we approached the front door under the covered porch after five weeks in Europe, we were greeted by a frantic rush of wings. We looked at where it had come from and saw in the corner of the porch near the window by my desk a beautifully made nest tucked into the stiff bristles of an upended broom. In the nest were two naked robin chicks and an egg.

Babies rule the world around them. For the next two weeks we had to approach the house quietly, entering not through the front door under the covered porch but through the French doors into the living room. And of course we couldn't sweep the covered porch or the deck with the broom. What we could do was watch the robin family as the young ones grew up. The brush was three feet from where I sat at my desk, but just out of sight until I moved, very slowly and quietly, up to the window and looked sideways out to see how they were doing. As soon as I showed myself, whichever parent was sitting there exploded off the nest, leaving the chicks looking at me.

They weren't tiny for long, and they weren't ever really cute, as so many other animal babies are. They were three wide open beaks supported somehow by insignificant straining bodies. If she had been working at my desk, Ann would have been beside herself, because every minute a parent would fly off the nest past the window, and every other minute a parent would fly back in with food in its beak. Each day the nest bulged with plumper, more feathery bodies, with bigger, even wider open beaks, until suddenly all was quiet. The nest was empty. Nothing flew in or out. It had been two weeks from egg to flight.

We missed having the family so close to our home, but that didn't stop me getting rid of the nest and putting the brush to its proper use, cleaning up feathers and droppings all over the covered porch. I put the nest on display in the garage and put the brush back where it had been, bristle side down this time. We think the robin parents built another nest in the dwarf blue spruce in our front deck border a few yards from the brush and had a second brood, but the tree's branches were so close together and its needles so thick, very broomlike, that I never managed to see a nest among them.

On the other side of the living room, to my left as I sit at my desk, the picture window looks out at lilacs with narcissi surrounding them in the spring and daylilies in summer; at the garage, with a bed to its right full of flowering plants; at the meadow, with the path leading through it to the bottom entrance to the west woods; and to the line of fourteen weeping willows bordering the west woods. Out in the meadow we may see deer, rabbits, or groundhogs browsing, turkeys pecking, or very occasionally a fox trotting purposefully in a particular direction. But close to the window are rhododendrons and a big crab apple, from one of whose boughs hangs a bird feeder, and that's where the activity never stops.

It would be fine if the only visitors to the bird feeder were cardinals (Mrs. is called Claudia, pronounced Cloudier, of course) and chickadees and tufted titmice and nuthatches and goldfinches and the other finches I can't identify. That would be fine, but bird feeders, as all bird feeder owners know, are chipmunk feeders and squirrel feeders too, and that's not so fine. Chipmunks we don't mind, but squirrels, at least when they are on or near the bird feeder, are the enemy, like Doreen.

Squirrels don't harm our plants as Doreen does, and they don't harm the birds, which often feed alongside them, but they do take over. They are almost the size of the feeder itself, and they eat up the food at a huge rate. Most bird feeders are touted as squirrelproof, but squirrels are smart; they find a way to unproof feeders. We get irrationally angry when we see one hanging there upside down, tucking into the food meant for the birds, and when we see two of them hanging there, we get doubly angry.

When a squirrel approaches the feeder, Ann is transformed. Her students wouldn't recognize her. "Don't you dare! Get out of it! Go on, get out of it!" And she jumps up and down and bangs on the window. When I see and hear all this, I think of the scene in the first book of Proust's *Remembrance of Things Past* when Marcel sees the servant Françoise with the chicken which she will present so beautifully the next day at dinner but which now she is trying to kill, cursing it with shrill cries of "Filthy creature! Filthy creature!"

Not that I can ignore those squirrels philosophically. I've spent money on a special mix of seeds guaranteed to attract songbirds, and this squirrel is gobbling up my money and their food. I just can't accept that squirrels, who spend their days trying to find a nut here and a seed there, should enjoy the bulk supply of each that I'm providing for the birds. It isn't quite as easy for them as if I had handed it to them on a plate, but it's easy enough if they hang upside down and poke their heads in at the openings. We yell at them, chase them off, and a minute later they're back for more.

Ann and I are television tennis junkies, and Wimbledon was particularly good in the summer of '04, but we found that Andy Roddick, Roger Federer, Serena Williams, and Maria Sharapova were competing not only with each other but with squirrels outside the picture window, a little to the left of the television, for our attention. There was charming feathery movement out there all day long, but when a gray shape larger than a bird was poised on a branch near the feeder, how could we concentrate on the game? Is it going to leap onto the feeder? What's the score? Should I get up and harass it? Love-forty? Who won that point? Oh no, I missed it. It became a real problem.

It got so bad in the middle of the summer that I brought a long stick into the living room and placed it next to the window nearest the bird feeder. I cranked open the window and took out the screen so I could poke the stick at the feeder. I put the screen back in because I didn't want bugs to fly in. The squirrel came back. I took the screen out again. The squirrel scurried off. I waited. It came back. I lunged. The stick wasn't quite long enough, so I never managed to touch the squirrel despite numerous attempts. And I never managed to keep the squirrel away. Ann smiled at my frustration because it was the same as hers, but if anyone else had seen me, they would have wondered: was this really how I spent my summer?

Why don't chipmunks annoy us? They are rodents too, and should be just as unwelcome at the bird's dinner table as squirrels. They are smaller and eat less than the squirrels, of course, but they are just as determined to get their fill. So determined, in fact, that half of their body disappears into the feeder when they eat, leaving only their back end visible. Ann laughs at them. It's the cuteness factor that softens our anger. They have cuter heads than squirrels, and that cute striping down their sides, and they seem to be having fun when they chase each other. I don't feel compelled to try to reach them with the stick.

The cuteness factor applies to the birds too. We like the tufted titmice, whose tufts go up and down like the cardinals', according to some prompting we can't understand, and the chickadees, which don't seem to mind how close we get to them. Blue jays are striking but not cute. They are much bigger than the tufted titmice and chickadees and finches, and their raucous shrieks near the feeder seem like the shouts of a bully. All I can say in favor of their noise and the noise of crows is, I would miss them terribly if I couldn't hear them anymore. They are good rowdy company.

Robins don't visit the feeder, but they certainly don't mind being close to human activity. Soon after the robins nested in our broom, I bought a Russian olive from Callander's. We arranged to have it delivered at the weekend, but at the weekend Callander's called to say that they didn't want to move it while robins were sitting on eggs in a nest in its branches. At the nursery, the ten-foot-high tree was right on the path that prospective buyers walk on, and there's a good deal of traffic there. In two weeks, the eggs had become fledglings, the fledglings had grown and flown, and Callander's delivered the tree with the empty nest in place. It's now in the upper lawn.

A pair of robins, maybe the ones that nested in that brush, like hopping around on the upper lawn. We watch them, and plenty of other action, from the kitchen and dining room. Judging by the amount and persistence of color, the back deck border has become our most successful bed. In the spring there's a bright line of narcissi in it, then lilies appear through dense greenery, then bright yellow rudbeckia and purple pink Echinacea, which one year flowered together for more than eight straight weeks. You can't keep your eyes away from them when you're washing the dishes. Swallowtail butterflies love the flowers, as do hummingbirds, and when the flower petals have faded and dropped, finches balance on their prickly hemispherical seedheads to peck out their seeds.

At the end of that thin strip of perennials I put a birdbath. I would like to know what guarantees that birds will visit a birdbath for a drink or a dip, because bird visits to ours are rare events. I wish they were routine, several times a day. When robins land on its edge, take a drink, then get in and swish around, that's when I know I can interrupt Ann at her work without annoying her. What's a train of thought compared to robins taking a dip on a hot day? Sometimes two robins are in the bath together. They look as if they're having a good time.

If Ann or I saw a bear out of the window, we would

let each other know pretty fast. We haven't seen one yet, but I think it's only a matter of time before we do. Bears are in the neighborhood — so many of them, in fact, that the *Independent,* our local newspaper, announced that they could no longer promise to acknowledge, let alone publish, photographs of them. Roberta and Viki have been visited. When Viki asked us recently whether we would like a drink and we replied with our usual, "Do bears shit in the woods?" (i.e., "Yes, we all know they do, and of course we want a drink. How can you ask?"), she said, "No, actually, they shit outside our window." A bear had wrecked the bird feeder outside their window and left a great claw scrape on their wall and a huge turd on the ground. Then, when a day or two later we walked around our own woods with them, Roberta kept pointing to turds which were larger than a dog's and wondering whether they were bears'. She promised to check them out in her reference book on the subject (a highly specialized work) and let us know.

I suppose like any other human I'll have mixed feelings about seeing a bear on the property. On the one hand, what an impressive animal! And if it has babies trooping along with it, how cute! But bears are scary, and mother bears with cubs are dangerous. I really don't want to feel scared in my own home. Unfortunately, bears love the seeds in a bird feeder, so if any are nearby, they may come right up to our picture window. I would rather see them at a safe distance: in the middle of the upper or lower lawn or at the edge of the woods. On the other hand, if they were just outside our windows, I might get a great photograph to send to Roger in England.

DESIGN

CHAPTER 14

Dreaming in Color

WHEN I TELL PEOPLE who don't garden that I garden, quite often they say, "Oh, vegetables?" and when I say no, they say, "Oh, flowers." If that isn't the end of the conversation, we may go on to talk about flowers we like: daffodils, roses, lilies, irises, and so on. The list of flowers I like is very long but, unless they are for some reason more than just interested, nongardeners' eyes are likely to glaze over if I go much further than the obvious ones, and I don't venture into topics such as perennials versus annuals, or the overall design of our garden, or my long-term plans for it. And I don't let on that flowers of any sort are unfortunately a rather insignificant feature in our garden, which might be puzzling and a downer. A show of colorful flowers is, after all, to a large extent what gardening is all about, isn't it?

We have fifteen perennial gardens now, so we have a lot of plants, many of which flower nicely if I am doing my job. But I consider all nine and a half acres at Ginger "garden," including its five acres of woods, to be integrated according to my long-term plan somehow with the remaining acres, which consist of lawn, trees, shrubs, buildings, and the perennial beds. The overall effect is pleasing, but wildly colorful it's not. I would love to be able to tell people that large sections of our garden are full of plants blooming perpetually in Technicolor: scarlet, blue, yellow, white, cream, pink, red, crimson, magenta, orange, purple, and as many variations and combinations of those colors as possible and as many shapes as possible. But that's a dream. The reality is largely shades and shapes of green and brown.

It's not only the quite small proportion of our acreage devoted to flowering perennials that accounts for the lack of brilliant color in our garden most of the time and not only the formidable economics of increasing the proportion. There's the climate. In New York's Columbia County, winter happens. For many months of our year nothing flowers, or rather, nothing with any noticeable color — hellebores are intriguing but not colorful, and snowdrops are endearing but make little impression unless massed in great quantities, which we don't have yet. Then, during many of the remaining months of the year, the warm flowering months, plants are — well, not flowering. They are either growing before they flower or forming seeds after they have flowered. And another thing: there's a big difference between flowers and plants. A peony is a showy flower, and there may be several flowers to a stem, and many stems to a plant, but the plant has much more greenery than it has pink or crimson flowers. A dozen roses in a vase make a fine yellow or white splash in a room, but on a bush in a garden they are so many blobs of color surrounded by green. When they aren't brown or white in winter, most gardens are mostly green most of the time.

And it works fine in most gardens, because an enclosed and designed space of greenery offers one of the great restorative experiences. Add the smell of mown grass or moist earth and the sound of birds and a few minutes of uninterrupted time and how can the soul not be calmed? Who needs those other colors?

But we do like flowers. Like the bees and the butterflies and the hummingbirds, we are drawn to them. Flowers are so much more interesting than leaves. No one gives a bouquet of greenery. Greenery added to a bouquet of flowers is free. Plants are objects of wonder, extraordinary self-sustaining contraptions, with their hidden roots finding water and nutrients and their leaves manufacturing energy from light and air, but their flowers are something else. If plants are the means by which genes propagate themselves, flowers are the most brilliant tactic in the gene's, or the plant's, strategy. They are the sensual, sexual part of the plant, although plants don't, as we do, woo each other directly. They use that magnificent color, those glorious smells, and those amazing shapes to lure go-betweens to pick up pollen and take it to other flowers of the same species. It just so happens that in the process they also lure humans to admire them extravagantly, to give them as gifts, to put them in vases, and to keep the plants that bear them growing healthily.

Humans even see human sensuality and sex in them — witness the paintings of Georgia O'Keeffe and the photographs of Edward Weston. But what, I think, we see more generally is faces, and I don't mean the configurations of color and shape that make us smile at pansies, for instance. On many annuals and perennials, a flower bears the same relationship to the rest of its green plant that a human face does to the rest of its body. It's the face that attracts us in a person, its animation, its interest, its beauty. If the person's body is great too, so much the better. The same with a plant, except that there is no such thing as an unattractive flower.

In the figure-ground relationship to be perceived in the ever-changing series of pictures that is our garden — changing week by week, but changing also as we walk around it — it is the flowering plants that are the figures set against the ground of the trees and shrubs and lawn and all the plants that are not flowering. It is the flowers our eyes seek as they wander over the shades of green everywhere; it is the flowers our eyes find and focus on. And even if there is little color provided by the few flowers in the overwhelmingly green garden, our eyes are satisfied. And even if in the long term it will be the structure of the place that will be remembered, in the short term it will be the flowers. Flowers are why we grow most of our plants, flowers are what we wait for during those flowerless months and then later are sad to see die. The more flowers the better: upright blue lupines, flat yellow yarrow, rounded pink saponaria — the more combinations of shape and color the better.

One of the great pleasures introduced by savvy entrepreneurs, mainly Korean, to the New York City and other city street scenes in the last twenty years has been the solid blocks of bright color of flowers for sale, crowded together and banked on the sidewalks in front of their markets. That's what I want our perennial beds to be like. Well, no I don't, because I live in reality, not dreamland. But I can't help looking at gardening books and magazines, and when I turn their pages and see their photographs, I can't help lingering on those amazing borders of colorful plants. Where are they? Are they in dreamland too? No, people with names created them, in places with addresses. Are they in our hardiness zone? I keep reading. Many of the plants described in the caption can be grown in zone 5. Maybe dreams such as these could be realized right here. I show the photos to Ann, and she points to the ones she particularly likes. Maybe I could make a long list of these plants, buy them by the dozen and half dozen, design for the best arrangement of colors, height, width, texture of foliage, and time of blooming, then prepare our soil, plant and mulch and water and wait and watch and — bingo: we'll have a glorious border of color all our own.

Some of the photographs in Hugh Johnson's *Principles of Gardening* show herbaceous borders to dream about. It's unfair, because his observations bring you back to the real world:

> The fully fledged herbaceous border, a massive bed filled entirely with hardy perennials, was a *tour de force* of the last decades of the nineteenth century and the first generation of the twentieth ... This grand manner was too grand to last. The "static rainbow" needed not only a consummate artist to design it but endless painstaking craftsmanship to keep it going. To hold all those perfectly graded plants in place a comprehensive system of corsetry was devised. To urge them to maximum performance they must be constantly lifted, divided, replanted, and fed. Furthermore, in their pure form such perfectly choreographed displays were generally and officially considered out of play for half the year. At a given moment in October the gardeners moved in to clear all the remnants of beauty away.

But it can be done even now, a hundred years later. Ruth and Leon's garden, five minutes from our own, started out as a bit of cleared woods and a stream, and in early July it is just as eye-popping as any in these magazines. They are two people, not twenty. But it did take many years, and those years consisted of days, and those days consisted of hours. When I visited them to pick up the *rugosa* roses they were digging out and giving to us last year for our garden, Ruth had clearly been kneeling among her plants since early in the day. I said that I bet she had been up since five-thirty in the morning. She said it was probably earlier than that.

Our garden has much more lawn and is generally much more green than Ruth and Leon's, but a list of the flowering plants in it would nevertheless be long. What flowers have been particularly satisfying? I suppose the ones I like best are the ones that signal from a distance and when I approach make me yell for Ann to come and look. These are generally about the size of my hand, give or take an inch or two, big enough, when we get close, to reveal an amazingly intricate structure and patterning. Oriental poppies, with brilliant scarlet petals thinner than tissue paper and coal-black centers; bearded irises, particularly the stunning sky-blue ones with the yellow track in the center; peonies, especially the lush, creamy white ones with a little spot or two of crimson near the center and the white ones with a yellow center, like sunny-side-up fried eggs; lilies, with the most sensual arrangement of pistil and stamens at the center of subtle-colored, curved, waxy petals; daylilies, shouting out their perfection of color and shape; big alliums with their unbelievably perfect small flowers in profusion creating together one perfectly beautiful sphere.

But how many flowers are not perfect when you look at them closely? Many of our narcissi are perfect. Our Siberian iris flowers, a wonderful blue, get rather lost among their leaves, and their color doesn't carry far, but look at them closely: they are perfect. Our 'Honorine Jobert' anemones, green centers surrounded by pale yellow at the center of a ring of white petals, are perfect. Rudbeckia, bright golden yellow daisies with a dark center — you see them everywhere in the fall, you can't get away from them — and Echinacea, with purple-pink petals drooping from a rounded center like the feathers on a badminton shuttlecock: look at their blooms individually and you see perfection. Dandelions are everywhere in our lawn, but look at a dandelion flower and who cares that it's a weed. It's a perfect flower.

Our garden has so much lawn, weeds and all, that in many places you can look across fifty yards of green, in some places a hundred. I feel I have succeeded as a gardener if I look around at the shrubs and young trees and the small perennial beds and nothing in the general prospect jars or jangles or makes me frown. But I also feel I have succeeded when I look at an individual flower in a garden and see perfection. Leaves can reward close study: look at the leaves of a bleeding heart. Whole plants can be superbly satisfying: bleeding heart, Russian sage, daylily, coral bells, lavender, santolina, catmint, teucrium. Gardens of grass and pachysandra and ivy and evergreen shrubs and trees can be lush and calming. But it is the colorful, varied flowers, especially on herbaceous plants, that gardeners dream about.

CHAPTER 15

Green

BECAUSE ALL PLANTS in the landscape use chlorophyll in their leaves to grow and keep themselves alive
(in the process keeping most animals alive, humans included), and because leaves take up the largest surface
area of most plants, and because chlorophyll is green,
the main color in the landscape and in any garden in
spring and summer is green. Most people, including
most gardeners (but excluding farmers and vegetable
gardeners), are fixated on the color, size, shape, and
smell of the sexual organs of plants instead of their energy factories, but the fact remains that the colors that
confront us during the growing season in the garden
are not red or purple or yellow or pink but shades of
green.

Green is the main color of nature, and green is the
background color of gardens in spring and summer.
Much of the time we don't pay attention to it. It's just
there, everywhere. We may notice the variations on the
color: at Ginger, for instance, the willows in summer
are a pale gray-green; the white pines' green is so dark
sometimes that it seems almost black; the spruce in our

front deck border has blue-green needles; and Ann likes to stroke the velvety silvery-green lamb's ears in the border by the garage. But plants colored like that are generally like buildings that may catch our attention briefly because they're not quite like all the other buildings on the block: interesting when we take the time to study them, but meanwhile not distracting us from the people on the sidewalk. In the garden, flower color is the action, green leaves merely the setting.

Humans have, naturally, evolved to be comfortable with green as the overall color of growing plants, although I suspect that not many people would say it's their favorite color. Humans seldom choose it to color their walls, floors, or ceilings unless it is so pale that the word "green" hardly comes to mind. I associate truly green floors and walls with corridors in unpleasant institutions, although I can't remember precisely which hospitals or barracks had them. Outside, you don't see green on a city street in winter: not on the buildings, not on billboards, not on posters — maybe a bit here or there on an awning, that's all. And one opinion I know all publishers' marketing directors share is that green is not a selling color for the jacket of a book. Looking at my own bookshelves, I see only a tiny fraction of them have green jackets or covers. But as a background color in the garden in spring and summer, green is just fine.

The time that I realize just how much I like green here in the Northeast is when I want it but can't have it, which is for too many months of the year. In winter here, the background color is white or gray and brown. White is the wonder of our world when we wake to it after an overnight snowfall, but it quickly palls, and the grays and browns of trunks and leafless branches are fascinating up to a point, a point I reach around mid-

January. It's about then that I start yearning for green, even though at that time of year I find it as difficult to imagine that what I am looking at will be clothed in green again in four months' time as it is to imagine myself semi-unclothed out there again. Allover green here means warmth and growth, which in January are a memory and a tantalizing dream.

Winter does have its compensations for a looker and learner, which is what I hope I will always be. You get to see all the differences in the structure of trees: how and where boughs branch from the trunk; how and where smaller branches angle away from bigger ones; ditto twigs. You can identify a tree just as surely by its distinctive winter silhouette as by the shape of its leaves in summer, with their distinctive veins and edges. I still find the distinctions difficult; also the differences in trunk color and texture. For me it is fascinating, but as daunting a subject as distinguishing the grasses in our meadow. It's as daunting a subject as cubism: not just figuring out whether particular paintings are by Picasso or Braque in 1910 and 1911 (even they found that difficult), but what the little individual lines and curves mean on their canvases and how they manage somehow, oddly, to represent a just-recognizable shape. I think I can understand why, when they were radically reworking the volume of objects on flat canvases in their epoch-making "analytical" cubist phase, they limited their palette to a very few muted colors, which were, coincidentally, the colors of deciduous plants in winter.

During 1910 and 1911, Picasso and Braque not only abandoned the colors of the summer landscape but they came indoors, as if from the cold of winter. Before those years, as we see at the beginning of the superb Museum of Modern Art publication *Picasso and Braque: Pioneer-*

ing Cubism, they were looking at landscapes and using the color green, but then it seems they needed to study subjects more conveniently at hand to solve the representational problems they had set themselves, obsessively cutting up the shapes of people, mandolins, pipes, jugs, guitars, cards, tables, glasses, bottles, vases, violins, clarinets, books, harps, knives, and forks and reassembling them in a whole new articulation of browns, grays, creams, and slanted lines and shadings on their canvases — as if such a rigorous intellectual exercise could not afford the distractions of bright summer colors. There's barely a landscape among them. It wasn't until the summer of 1912, in their "synthetic" cubist phase, that a little pink or light blue crept back onto their canvases, and it wasn't until 1914, at least as shown by the last color photograph in the book, that a brighter color was allowed to dominate one of their canvases. It wasn't a landscape, it was a girl; but the overall color (at last!) was bright green.

The overall color of spring is light, bright green, bringing with it relief and excitement. Then gradually it darkens to become the background color again, and other colors grab our attention. What we appreciate in our greens is signs of vigorous health rather than subtle distinctions in their richness or brilliance or softness or even hue. But unless we are trained artists, we aren't likely to have the eyes of a Gertrude Jekyll, who, in *Home and Garden,* describes sitting down one day, tired, on the lowest steps leading into her rock garden, half-lazily picking up a leaf of lady's mantle beneath her and finding "how much, besides the well-known beauty of its satin back, there was to admire in it. The satin lining, as is plain to see, comes up and over the front edge of the leaf with a brightness that looks like polished silver against the dull green surface." And then she proceeds to devote a whole page to examining the leaf in detail.

The structural details of a plant and the texture of its leaves may help account for its particular variety of green. But there are other factors, such as time of day, quality of light, atmosphere, and distance. In another passage of the same book, Jekyll describes the differences among all the greens our untrained eyes tend to see as the same color: "I remember driving with a friend of more than ordinary intelligence, who stoutly maintained that he saw the distant wooded hill quite as green as the near hedge. He knew it was green and could not see it otherwise, till I stopped at a place where a part of the face, but none of the sky-bounded edge, of the wooded distance showed through a tiny opening among the near green bushes, when to his immense surprise, he saw that it was blue."

For most of the summer, my garden of groundcovers on the slope in the east woods — when it fills out, and only if I can keep it weeded — should display stripes of different greens. The best example I know of the effect I would like it to produce, an unattainable model, is in the central Italian section of the Conservatory Garden in Central Park. Its plan is churchlike. When you enter it through imposing gates on Fifth Avenue, you see on either side of you allées of crab apples (the aisles), you look ahead over a fine lawn (the nave) over a fountain (the altar) up to the enclosing curve of an iron pergola festooned with wisteria (the pillars of the apse). But below the pergola and between the fountain and the pergola, corresponding to an ambulatory in a church, you see five clipped concentric hedges rising one above the other in different shades of green: dark green yew alternating with gray-green spiraea.

I'll never be able to get my edges crisp like that, but it's worth a try. And I'll have to keep weeding out individually beautiful wildflowers, such as phlox and bellflowers, and one of my arch-enemies, garlic mustard, in order to keep the bands of green low, without upright punctuations of pink and white and purple and blue all over the place, but that too should be worth it. When I e-mailed our friend Dorothy James about making do with green, or rather making the most of green, she e-mailed back: "In Parklands, the little Welsh estate where my father was, one of his neighbors planted an entirely green garden — different shades of green, of course. You know how English gardens are — absolutely choc-a-bloc with flowering annuals — well, some of them on that little circle where his house was were quite overdone, I thought, with hanging baskets at every turn, etc., and maybe this neighbor was rebelling against that. At any rate, her garden was the loveliest garden in Parklands."

"Lovely" is the word the speaker in Andrew Marvell's "The Garden" (1681) uses about the color green, as he finds rest and quiet among a garden's trees and flowers and sinks into its sensuality:

> No white nor red was ever seen
> So amorous as this lovely green.

The poem, arguably the greatest garden poem in the language, rises to a climax as the speaker's mind withdraws from "pleasure less" into happiness and in an act of transcendence creates "far other worlds and other seas,"

> Annihilating all that's made
> To a green thought in a green shade.

I understand this completely without quite under-
standing it, which I find often to be the case with poetry,
but I do believe that a feeling I recognize (being "one
with nature" is one way of describing it) has never been
described better. Then, in an extraordinary vision, the
speaker sees his soul flying up from ground level like a
bird into the boughs of a tree:

> Here at the fountain's sliding foot,
> Or at some fruit-tree's mossy root,
> Casting the body's vest aside,
> My soul into the boughs does glide;
> There, like a bird it sits and sings,
> Then whets and combs its silver wings,
> And, till prepared for longer flight,
> Waves in its plumes the various light.

This is language from another century and another
country, so to speak: I don't believe in the existence of a
soul, and the idea of its gliding into the boughs of a tree
like a bird is bizarre. But these central stanzas of a poem
by a sixty-year-old Yorkshireman speak to something
in me, to what I could call my innermost core, and of
course to my gardening self, more intensely than almost any others I can think of (well, there are Blake and
Wordsworth and Keats) and even more directly than
the ecstatic lines of W. B. Yeats's great poem "Sailing to
Byzantium" (1928), in which at the age of sixty-three he
(or his speaker) prays, surely remembering Marvell's
poem, that his soul, translated "out of nature," may take
the form of an artificial gold bird singing on a golden
bough.

There's no green in Yeats's poem, but Dylan Thomas
uses "green" six times in six stanzas to describe the ec-

stasy of his happy youth in a country paradise in his "Fern Hill" (1946). Thomas's reading of this poem, fortunately preserved for all time, was one of the great experiences of my early literary life, and I still think the poem is a masterpiece of intricate sounds and poignant ideas. He also uses "gold" (Yeats's color) four times and "lovely" (Marvell's term) twice in his virtuoso celebration of youth's carefree rapture, now lost forever to time.

When these transcendental poems use specific religious imagery, they don't speak to me. I wish, for instance, that Marvell hadn't felt obliged to introduce the silly notion, surely even then a dead convention, that paradise was best enjoyed by "man . . . without a mate" (presumably because Eve brought evil into the world?). Nevertheless, as a nonreligious nature lover who understands how a lawn and trees and perennials and the sound of bees and birds can induce a mystical trance, I respond wholeheartedly to Marvell's poem about a garden and Thomas's poem about the country around his aunt's house. For me, most of Marvell's nine stanzas capture convincingly how seductive a lush green garden can be, touching the senses, the mind, and, yes, the soul (which, even if nonexistent, I know Beethoven's music, cared-for gardens, and successful poems are good for).

Ginger's land slopes down toward the north, which means that snow stays longer on its lawn than on any other lawns around here. That's not so great in the late winter when I want to see the green that all our neighbors are seeing. But the combination of north-facing slope and heavy clay soil does bring us one advantage later in the year: our lawn stays wetter and greener than our neighbors'. It's better to look at, if not to walk on, than theirs. Of course, when droughts hit the area, the grass will always be greener where irrigation systems have been installed; the grass will always be proverbially greener in more wealthy properties or longer-cared-for properties than at Ginger; and the grass of childhood and youth will always be proverbially greener than the grass of our present age, which is why Dylan Thomas's poem strikes so universally resonant a chord, and maybe why Acaster Manor's garden and the Yorkshire moors still pull so hard on my imagination. But the pleasing fact remains: in dry summers, the grass is not proverbially but literally greener at Ginger.

What if the leaves of our grass and perennials and shrubs and trees weren't green but, say, blue or yellow or neon pink or phosphorescent orange? Well, Andy Warhol gave us a glimpse of what our scenery would look like in his spectacular portfolio of ten "Flower" screenprints. If anything is, or ever was, outrageous in these pictures, it surely isn't or wasn't the color of the flowers, which it is easy to imagine having been grown that way, or their flatness, which is the result of the enlargement of a photograph — or the out-of-register printing of two of them — which merely draws attention to the silkscreen process. It's the color of the grass in five of them: two of them blue, one yellow, one neon pink, and one phosphorescent orange. Even at sunset, or sunrise with silvery dew on it, I never expect to see grass like that out of our windows at Ginger, or anywhere else, with my earthbound eyes. Would I like it? I like looking at it under and around those Warhol flowers.

And as for the leaves of plants above grass level, in this part of the country we have only to wait for a year when the conditions are right for the fall to reveal all those totally improbable but splendidly inevitable colors as chlorophyll disappears and carotene and anthocyanine remain. It's a blast: not just yellow and scarlet but pink and crimson and orange and lemon and purple and blue. As Hugh Johnson says about fall, "Whole trees are the color of our most vivid flowers." And like vivid flowers, one tree may sport a single bright color, another tree a different bright color, and another a whole range of them.

Just how brilliant fall color can be is, for me, best shown, not by familiar long-distance photographs of hillsides or even by a closeup of a leaf, but in some of Andy Goldsworthy's photographs commemorating the passage of time: bright yellow elm leaves held together with water in a highly artificial pattern — say, a rectangle — against the contrasting dull winter colors of long-dead leaves and twigs on a forest floor; or bright scarlet maple leaves laid sharp end up in a long thin line along the tops of large smooth gray boulders like the spiky ridge on a dark gray dinosaur's back. You look at those leaves and you think, can those colors be real? But then you see that this artist, for me the best visual poet of time's behavior in the natural world since Monet, has photographed them a day later and the colors are fading, then again a day or two later, and they are dead or gone.

I can't help having mixed feelings about all the color at Ginger in the fall. On the one hand, it's the best show the place puts on, far superior to anything I have ever coaxed from the perennials nearer to earth. The background scenery steals the show. On the other hand, during spring and summer I don't look forward to it as I look forward to green during winter. And when fall arrives, it's always too soon. Surrounded by all that exuberant color, I'm only too conscious that soon I'll be looking around at gray and brown. I'll be cold and I'll be looking forward again to green.

CHAPTER 16

Masculine Flowers

EMILY E-MAILED ME with a question: "I'm trying to remember the name of a plant that we used to have in pots. It's what I would consider a masculine plant — big and bristly, with red or white flowers, and kind of whitish stalks, and shiny leaves, and I think it smelled bad. Each flower is about four inches in diameter, a sphere (not flat like a daisy) with round petals all over the place. Do you know the one I'm talking about? Maybe it starts with a G or a C." I couldn't think what it was, and neither could Ann. A few hours later, Emily called. The name had suddenly come to her: geranium. Right, right, right, I remember. We did have geraniums (actual name pelargoniums), with red or white flowers (actually clusters of flowers which often form spheres) in our Brooklyn co-op apartment years ago. Their leaves aren't shiny, and they don't smell bad — they smell great — but that mention of the smell should have tipped me off. Ann and Emily and Lucy thought they smelled bad. But why did she want to remember this plant, and what's this about masculine? She said that a friend wanted a plant for his window box, but it had to be a masculine plant, not a girlie plant.

A masculine plant. Geranium. Hmmm. Well, I can see that geraniums could be considered more masculine than, say, pansies, some of which have soft facelike flowers, and have that name. And more masculine than the small relatives of the pansy, Johnny Jump Ups, which could definitely be accused of being cute little things, despite their name. But still, I wouldn't have thought of geraniums as especially masculine. There is the matter of the smell, of course, which I liked and the women didn't. Maybe that was it. Did her friend want a plant whose smell women couldn't possibly confuse with cologne?

What other plants could Emily suggest to her friend? The question made me wonder whether I don't in a sense consider all flowers more feminine than masculine. I think maybe I do. Biologically, most flowers have male and female sexual parts, but that's not the point. How about marigolds, a good hearty orange, with a smell that keeps away insects? They're tough. Several orange marigolds and several scarlet salvia: that would be a non-sissy combination. Or if all flowers are feminine, maybe he should go for something that hardly ever flowers. A big spiny cactus. No, a desert plant wouldn't survive in a New York City window box; it's not tough enough. Cactuses here need to be coddled indoors.

What about Jack-in-the-pulpit (*Arisaema triphyllum*)? I am fascinated by this plant, perhaps because it is so different from most of the other plants I grow. Its "flower" (which just doesn't seem to be the right term) is in no way a pretty arrangement of petals or soft colors — quite the opposite. It's not colorful, and its shape is positively weird: a fleshy upright spike with a sheath around its sides and back and coming up over its top. This is succeeded in the fall by brilliant scarlet berries surrounding a stout stem. I wonder whether anyone has ever tried growing this wildflower in a window box. It would need to be in the shade. We have lots of them in our woods at Ginger.

Talking of stout stems, there's an even better candidate, again provided it can be grown in such a place. It's not a flowering plant but a mushroom, the stinkhorn (*Phallus impudicus*). It's all stem. It's fairly common in the Northeast, but in the wild, and it's certainly not sold for its ornamental qualities or for its fragrance. In fact, I bet it isn't sold at all. If Emily's friend manages to plant one, he'll have something startling to show off when it starts to grow. A thick shaft thrusts up fast out of the earth, up to ten inches long in a few hours, complete with a rounded head covered in dark slime which gives off a foul stink and attracts flies, and then the whole thing dies down fairly quickly. I come across these occasionally in their decaying state in our woods. Would several of those be masculine enough?

Well, maybe he should stick with those bright annuals: marigolds and salvia, or the plant Emily first thought of, geraniums, or all three together. They are easy to buy, easy to grow, producing lots of bright color for a long time, and the marigold's and geranium's leaves will smell good or bad, depending on something or other — who you are, I guess.

CHAPTER 17

A Little Bright Red Is Enough

FOR MANY MONTHS last winter we had a bit of red balloon caught in the branches high up in the weeping willow at the center of our property. It was very conspicuous in the bare branches, and Ann and I kept thinking it was a cardinal until we saw again that it was only a piece of rubber the same size and color as a cardinal. It wasn't big enough to be an eyesore, like those dirty plastic bags that get caught in city trees, and I rather liked the thought that it was the last colorful remnant of a party in a neighbor's yard in a warmer season. Anyway, when the tree leafed out again in the spring, we wouldn't see it.

Then early one morning when I was looking at the tangle of shrubs at the west border of the upper lawn I saw another bright red blob, and I thought, oh no, one of those things is enough, we really don't need bits of red rubber caught in trees and shrubs all over the property, and I went up to disentangle it. When I came near, it flew off. This one really was a cardinal, and wherever it landed in the gray winter scenery it looked good. It called, and its voice was as penetrating and assertive (and to me as exciting) as its color. Spring wasn't far off.

Red can be very attractive, but I wouldn't want too much of it. What if all birds were red? And the same with plants: what if the leaves of all plants were red instead of green? Not just the grass in the lawn, which Andy Warhol has imagined for us, but the trees and shrubs, the herbaceous plants, all red? I have to close my eyes to imagine it. If I opened my eyes one day to a red-leafed lawn and red-leafed landscape, I would need to close them against the brightness.

I have added a dash of permanent bright red to the middle of our lower lawn, but only a dash. Among the various things the previous owners left, along with swimming pool furniture, bookshelves, and the "Willow Hill" bathroom towels, was a ship's air intake funnel, a large object that would have been heavy and awkward to carry to the dump. I painted the outside a high-gloss white and the throat bright shiny red, and set it in the middle of the lower lawn. It's our bit of crass artificiality in the garden, a feature somewhere between a sculpture and a plastic pink flamingo.

Otherwise, the only other permanent splashes of red around here are just off our property, at the very edge. I saw them later that same morning as I was walking through the west woods. There was a red plastic square tacked onto a tree just the other side of the low stone wall marking the property line. The red square carried a warning in big black letters that if I walked beyond that tree, I would be trespassing and would be prosecuted. As I walked along our side of the wall, I came to another bright red square on another tree, then another, another, and another. Two would have been enough to make it clear that the wall was the property line. I suppose it was hunters that were being warned, not me, but for most of the year that line of bright red squares would be intruding visually deep into our property. Unless I plant evergreens there, they would be masked by foliage only in spring and summer.

A little red goes a long way. Much more goes too far. Thousands of wild poppies in a field are beautiful because there's so much green still there, and while an acre of cultivated red tulips is a "wow" phenomenon, it's the poppies I would look at again and again, not the tulips. Nor would I want to keep looking at a large bed of nothing but scarlet salvias. I would be delighted to see a few more of the bright red oriental poppies that flower in our garden in early summer, but what I would really like is for our plants to flower for a little longer than they do. Every day after their green balls have unfolded and before they have become brown seed heads, Ann enthuses at the tissue paper delicacy of their garish scarlet petals.

The afternoon after I had been warned to stay on my side of the stone wall, I heard a woodpecker hammering away at a dead elm near where I had first seen the cardinal. It was a pileated woodpecker. I got Ann to look at it through binoculars: the size of a crow, big sharp light-colored beak, black and white stripe across its head and down its neck, bright red crest on the top of its head. It dug into the dead elm for at least an hour, then moved to a living willow. There it dug hole after hole for another half hour. Ann and I were busy doing other things, but we couldn't resist coming back to the window with the binoculars to watch all that strenuous work with its neck muscles and beak, and as we watched it was joined by a mate. The two of them dug beneath the willow bark a foot or so from each other. One of them would sometimes disappear around the other side of the tree, then the other, but we could see wood chips flying off sideways from the trunk, so we knew where they were. Then a splash of red would appear again, jabbing at the side of the tree trunk. Then the whole bird would come around to our side and the other would join it again.

I have to assume that the willow, which I had thought was healthy enough, has insects under its bark, and the birds will be back for more. There were two big holes at the back of the dead elm, but there are also big holes in living trees all over the property. It's sobering to think that all those trees are riddled with insects, but we're not unhappy that we have a resident or at least local pair of pileated woodpeckers determined to get at them. They're magnificent birds. What bodies, built to cling to the trunk of a tree while they bang into its bark and underlying wood with their beaks, hour after hour, tossing three-inch-long wood chips down as they dig for insects. But it's their size and their white-striped head and neck and especially their flaming red crest that keep us looking at them. The red is a big part of its attraction, but it's a small part of the bird.

CHAPTER 18

Thin Straight Lines

ON OUR FRIEND GEORGE'S recommendation, we
went to buy some irises from an iris specialist. Ann consulted the map as we drove for an hour through unfamiliar country. Roads gradually narrowed, until finally
at several intersections we spotted hand-painted plac-
ards with BAIRD'S IRISES and an arrow on them. At the
last placard we turned off the dirt road into a private
drive and parked by a building with no irises, no garden,
no people visible, just the silence of deep countryside. A
gap in a straggly hedge nearby led to an open area, and
in a few steps we knew we had come to the right place.
We were at the bottom of a large sloping field, and there,
stretching up the middle of the field above us, were two
long parallel lines of blazing color: irises, all in full
bloom. We had never seen so many iris plants, let alone
different varieties of iris.

Bruce Baird, who had been digging up at the top of
the field, planted his spade in the soil and came down to
greet us. He grows over two hundred varieties of iris for
himself and for the Central Hudson Iris Society, and
when they are dormant he divides them and sells some

at a very reasonable price. But he had suggested we come now, while they were all in bloom, so we would know what we would be getting if we wanted to order some. We walked up and down the long lines of color, and Bruce talked about each variety as we came to it. He told us which ones were new, which ones were fashionable, and which ones were particularly tough. Some people like near-black irises, some like yellow, some like brown, some like two-colored ones. Bruce pointed out his favorites, Ann had her favorites, and I had mine. We ordered some plants and wrote down their names, including 'Great Gatsby', 'Lady Friend', 'Black Hills Gold', 'Edith Poldark', 'Gypsy Romance', and 'Prestige Item'. What I didn't write down was a description of each and I didn't photograph them, so I have forgotten them already, and we will be awaiting their blooming with interest.

Bruce warned us not to expect all irises to bloom the first year, and I will be happy if over fifty percent of them flower well after two or three years. But what I took away that day wasn't just the prospect of some beautiful plants in our perennial beds; it was the memory of those two lines of plants. If there had been two hundred rows, each devoted to one variety of iris, I might have been turned off — photographs of massive, hot-colored tulip fields in Holland leave me cold — but those two multicolored strips, framed by the green field, were a revelation. Not that Bruce had any thought of impressing visitors with the design of his beds, which is strictly utilitarian. He is interested in the welfare of each individual plant and the differences among them. He works by himself, so two rows are all that he can handle. He keeps them narrow so that he can reach plants easily without stepping on others, and visitors can look at the plants closely to choose among them. New varieties get added at the top or bottom or wherever there are gaps: no planting by color or size, no thought of their arrangement to create a harmonious whole. He edges the beds not for aesthetic effect but to keep out weeds. He doesn't mow his field low to make it lawn. And yet it was the very simplicity of those long straight lines, and the very randomness of the colors that filled them, that made them such a memorable picture.

At Ginger we have a lot of open lawn which gets plenty of sun every day. Our perennial beds, on the other hand, are all partially shaded, and for a long time I wondered whether some at least of the perennials wouldn't be better off in the middle of the lawn. But then if I were to move them into the lawn, what shape of garden would I make for them? Square, rectangular, circular, elliptical? My vague thoughts were no more than that: I wasn't planning to interrupt the expanse of lawn, which we liked as it was. The new irises were going to go into existing beds. But I think these vague thoughts did make me especially interested in what could look very good in the middle of a field or lawn. A thin straight line of color could be great.

Anne Raver wrote a story in the *New York Times* (October 17, 2002) about Kurt Bloemel, "king of ornamental grasses." One of the accompanying photographs showed one long, bold brushstroke of red and several smaller dabs of red across a lawn. It was a carefully maintained planting of Japanese Blood Grass (which Bloemel had renamed Red Baron) and nothing else. The effect was dramatic, and in this case it was deliberate: there was an elegant bench in the background where people could sit and take it in. At the time I wondered how Red Baron would look splashed across Ginger's lower lawn, but it's not hardy enough to grow well in zone 5. However (file for future thought), other grasses might work well, even if they aren't as bright as Red Baron.

Our daily drive on the dirt road into Chatham takes us past Jack Millard's house, on the right. He has a lawn between his house and the road, and in the lawn, set back several yards from the road and parallel with it, is a thirty-foot line of peonies. It's what you see before you see his house or anything else on his property. The peonies are close together but only one plant deep. When they flower pink and white in the late spring, that straight line is one of the most pleasant sights in the area. Then, when the flowers die and their messy heads are cut off, it remains pleasant until late fall, a line of lush dark green foliage against the light green of the lawn.

How often do you see thin straight lines of annuals or perennials like that in a lawn? Hedges and perennial beds, yes, if they are close to and parallel to a wall or path or fence; but in a lawn, no, you don't see them, or at least I haven't seen them. A line of irises wouldn't be colorful for long, and there are better leaves than iris leaves for much of the year, but the contrast between their spiky leaves and a relatively smooth lawn could work.

This year I tried out a variation on the idea. I had to move a lot of Siberian irises, and I also had to divide some bearded irises. A spot toward the top of the upper lawn gets plenty of sun and shouldn't be too damp. I started taking off a strip of sod from the lawn up there, checked how the irises would look from the bench at the top of the lawn, and thought a thin line of them could look good. Then, as I sat on the bench looking at the line, I thought a gentle curve to the line would make it look better. I needed to divide some yucca at the same time, so I interspersed stretches of irises with yucca, which also has spiky leaves. We'll see how it works out, but it looks fine so far, without any plant having flowered. It's not a thin straight line — it's a thin curved line, a crescent, in the lawn.

CHAPTER 19

Sitting and Siting

ONE OF THE BEST WAYS to experience a garden is in the sitting position, and I'm planning to do more and more of it. When we bought Ginger, among the things we were happy to inherit from the previous owners were two heavy, utilitarian benches, of the sort you see in parks or on main streets, and two ancient Adirondack chairs. The benches are not bad to look at, but the wooden planks connecting their concrete sides to make their seats and backs are too thin and far apart for our rear ends to be truly comfortable, so we don't sit on them much. We left them where they were, one at the east edge of the upper lawn, the other at the west edge of the upper lawn, near the spectacularly shaped old apple tree which was then hidden by weedy shrubs. Those were two good sites, and later I spent a lot of time gardening around each of them.

We put the Adirondack chairs in the middle of this upper lawn, and in those first months we liked to sit in them with a drink in the evening and look down at the place we had bought, something we don't do so often now, even though their seats and backs are inclined at just the right angle for a weary body, and their wide, flat armrests easily accommodate a book or a drink. An absolute requirement for benches, chairs, and seats of any sort is that they themselves sit on level ground, which is something I failed to provide for these chairs, probably because I wasn't sure whether this should be their permanent position. As a result, sitting on them stressed their joints unequally, and they reached an advanced stage of ricketiness: they were about to disintegrate. Meanwhile, though, robins liked to perch on their backs and Ann liked to see them doing it from our kitchen, although their droppings, which I tended to forget to clean off, were a big disincentive for her to sit there. Still, the seats looked interesting from the house. One visitor looked up at them on a snowy evening and asked why we had a couple of tombstones up there.

While we were deciding what to do with the Adirondack chairs, we added benches elsewhere on the property, and I came to realize just how much the new and old ones contributed to the look of the place and to how we experienced it. Our parklike property was conducive to walking, stopping, and looking across lawn at specimen trees, distant perennial beds, and the sky. When we saw a red sky in the evening in our first year, we would take our drinks not up to the Adirondack chairs but down from the front of the house to a spot at the east edge of the lower lawn. There we could look across the lower lawn to a gap in the west wood trees beyond the lawn and the meadow, the perfect frame for whatever show the sky put on: pink, crimson, orange, scarlet, purple — color after color, then dark. It was a romantic spot, but we couldn't sit and linger. There wasn't a seat or bench. Another place we liked to go when Ann

needed a break from her desk and I from gardening was
down to the bottom of the lower lawn, to look back up
at the house. But the same thing applied: standing room
only; no seats for the audience.

Gardens are to be enjoyed; otherwise, what are we
laboring at? One way to enjoy a garden is to look at it.
Another, better way is to look at it, then walk around it,
feeling its textures with feet and fingertips, smelling it
here and there, and hearing what's going on among its
leaves and blossoms. But an even better way is to look
at it, walk around it, then sit down — you don't have to
be tired — and let its essence seep deeper and deeper
into your consciousness. For that you need something
to sit on.

Even the smallest garden surely needs a bench or a
seat. Large gardens need several. Considering that I
thought of our whole property as "garden," I quickly felt
that the large open part of our property needed more
seats than the four on our upper lawn. Even the upper
lawn could use another one. Ann liked to go up past the
Adirondack chairs to the top of the upper lawn to look
back down over the chairs, over the house, over the
lower lawn, over the trees in the middle distance, to the
horizontal strip of the Berkshires, just visible on clear
days many miles away. It was an obvious place to linger,
but again, no seat.

Seats in a garden have several functions:

- to look good in themselves,
- to look good in context (as focal points in a large
    picture),
- to feel good,
- and to provide particularly good views of the rest
    of the garden.

In a large garden, if there happen to be interesting plants nearby to inspect closely or to smell, so much the better, but merely as elements in its overall geometry or as items in its overall experience, seats are as powerful as specimen trees or statues or fountains. And like paths and arches and gates they signal their own special message about the garden as a whole. The very existence and positioning of a seat says, "Come over here and sit for a time and relax. There's a good view of the place from this spot." In a small garden it's a close view, in a large garden it's a longer view, but it may offer a close view too.

On Michelin maps a place with a good view gets a little three-line fan-shaped symbol showing the direction of the view, and a panorama gets three fan symbols arranged around a central point. That's the way I would show our seats if I were to draw a good plan of our garden: with little seat icons, each with a fan symbol showing which direction it looks. None of the individual perennial beds in the central area are quite as pleasing yet (however hard I have worked on them, and however beautiful the various plants in them) as the long view, the big picture of the whole garden from several different places. Why not mark those places with a seat?

So we did. We ordered two small benches for twenty-five dollars each from a carpenter nearby and another, larger one for fifty dollars. For the two smaller ones, the carpenter scooped a semicircular notch in the ends of two bits of thick tree trunk (the legs), then split another bit of trunk down the middle. The curved outside part of this piece fit into the notches of the legs; the flat interior part we sat on. They were easy to carry around in three separate pieces and easy to bang together. Not that we needed to do either. The site in each case was right, so they stayed where we put them, and the pieces fit snugly together without a need for nails or screws. We put the small benches at places we had liked to go to together: the sunset-viewing spot, and the bottom of the lower lawn. The larger bench, which differs from the smaller ones only in having a long plank — instead of a split trunk — fitting into rectangular notches in the legs, we set on the rock at the high place in the west woods. It's perched where two paths meet, and you can see it from a distance as you climb up them, a fine destination point with a good view back through the cleaned-up trees out to the open area.

Then came a gradual process of site upgrading, or garden creation, around the seats. The concrete-sided bench on the east edge of the upper lawn now has a semicircle of stones around it and a so far somewhat scrappy bed of daffodils in the spring and coreopsis and daylilies in the summer — strong yellows, in each case, to be seen from the distance of the house. The concrete-sided bench on the right is near the main entrance to the west woods, with, on one side, the wonderfully shaped apple tree I had revealed by clearing the weedy shrubs around it, and on the other, the ornamental grasses I had moved to stand like pillars signaling the entrance into the woods. I planted narcissi under the apple. Both of these concrete bench sites are worth developing further and are items for my annual list of projects. As for the sunset-view bench, I spent over three years transforming the site into a sloping garden of groundcover stripes.

You get what you pay for, and the twenty-five-dollar benches started to deteriorate at an early age: ants were eating away at their legs. When I asked Roger, on his next visit from Acaster, to help me design and make a couple of benches to be more permanent replacements, he promptly designed them and made them himself. They look good, and have a nice curve for your bottom to rest in, and softened edges at the front and back which feel good. We dug them in, and I am sure they will last for years. I moved the twenty-five-dollar benches, which have a year or two left in them, one to the place at the very top of the property where Ann tries to glimpse the Berkshires and we can now look at the curved line of irises, the other to another vantage point on the lower lawn by the meadow.

If our seats indicate good sightlines, the state of the seats, I have recently realized, may be an indication of how I perceive the progress of my gardening. A good site deserves a seat and gets it, then the site and seat deserve a garden. Then the site and garden deserve a better seat, and so on. I don't plan to add more seats — well, perhaps one or two over time — but I do plan to do enough to the areas around each seat to make close views from them as interesting as the long views. And I plan to upgrade a seat whenever a site deserves it. When the twenty-five-dollar benches collapse, we'll replace them with better ones. And I think I have a way to make those concrete-sided benches more comfortable. Wider planks. If they have notched ends, wider planks should fit into the holes in the concrete sides. They too are an annual list project. This time I should do them myself and not wait for Roger's next visit.

CHAPTER 20

The Long View

I HAVEN'T PAID much attention to the somewhat anonymous trees in our woods, other than clearing a lot of them out and pruning the lower branches of many of those remaining. And I haven't paid much more attention to the trees that were planted specifically to be looked at in the lawn. They don't seem to demand the care I lavish on the much smaller plants that die back in the fall, vanish in the winter, and come up again in the spring. I try to protect the trees from Doreen, and I relieve them of as much of their deadwood as I can reach, but otherwise I just let them stand there, and I take for granted that they will stick around forever, like old friends.

But friendship has to be worked at, and perhaps a different perspective is in order for a property like this. As we walk around Ginger, the typical view is the long view. Perennials may catch our eye when they are nearby and in flower, but more often we are looking across lawn at woods in the middle to far distance and at solitary trees in the lawn between us and the woods. When we sit on any of the benches, it is the larger features of the place that our eyes rest on, particularly the shapes and colors of the trees. A brown-purple–leaved Japanese maple near the house and next to it a Kousa dogwood, all white when it's in flower; white-flowering crab apples in the upper lawn and pink ones below the house; a huge white pine in the upper lawn, dark green all year; and red maples, one in the upper lawn, three in the lower lawn, bright red in the fall. The line of fourteen willows on the west edge of the meadow turn bright yellow when they catch the early morning sun. Ann points to them as soon as she is up for breakfast. All these familiar presences deserve more than regular happy acknowledgment. How healthy are they? How beautiful will they be in coming decades? How long will they last?

They are, after all, the biggest living things on the property, and they will keep growing. Taking the long view, I have to remember that they will become more and more difficult to move, and more and more difficult, emotionally and practically, to kill, if it ever came to that. Most of these big basic components of Ginger's landscape will outlast us, bringing delight or problems to others, but meanwhile, are they the right ones, the ones we want to be looking at for many years? For instance, those large dark evergreen shapes, white pine and eastern hemlock, near the south side of the house. Yes, they're superb, although they are a little too close for complete comfort in a storm. The two old crab apples, dark pink at the northeast corner of the house, brighter pink near the swimming pool, are wonderful when they flower, but they lose their leaves in wet summers. The young ash in the lower lawn: will it be the best tree for its position when it's huge? It doesn't do much for me, and it's at the very center of the view down from the house. I've never considered chopping it down or replacing it. Should I? The red maple in the lower lawn is magnificent in the fall, but the apples at the edge of the lower lawn beyond it don't flower much and look as if they may be dying. Shouldn't we plant some pink-flowering crab apples or plums down there for future owners? And over there by the meadow, shouldn't we plant not one but several examples of a fine species?

But trees are not the easiest things to think about and deal with. They start by challenging the imagination even before we have planted them: I find it very difficult to imagine, while they are still small, what the really big ones will look like decades from now, and how they will affect the look of the whole place when they're full-grown. So siting them is a problem. Then, when they are sited and dug in and settled, I must protect them from Doreen until they have grown out of deer-reach, which means that for much, perhaps all, of the year, and for many years, I must spray them with a succession of different disgusting-smelling liquids in rotation so Doreen doesn't get used to them, or I must stake and fence them, making them long-lasting eyesores. Then, when they are maturing, things start happening to them which we do or don't notice. The five arborvitae planted to hide the shed for the swimming pool pump were so badly eaten by Doreen that they in turn had to be hidden by Japanese pierises and Vanhoutte spiraeas, which Doreen doesn't like (so far). The large maple in the upper lawn lost leaves on its top branches in a dry summer, and those branches died. A sugar maple in the upper lawn has been so stressed that although tall, it has remained skinny and hasn't managed to grow anything longer than tiny twigs and leaves on its branches. A red cedar near the entrance to the driveway is covered every year with cedar apple rust: orange galls with gross, jellylike horns. I think this disease is weakening, perhaps killing, the apple trees near it.

But my efforts to grow young trees have so far not paid off. The Arbor Day Foundation sent me two years ago, in return for my ten-dollar membership fee, ten eighteen-inch-long trees thinner than a pencil. I sited them carefully, prepared the soil carefully, and staked and netted them. All died. My fault, I suppose. Meanwhile I see that three young trees — I think hawthorns, but I have to check — have sprung up with no help from me in the meadow we didn't cut last year. If they aren't weedy trees, I will let them grow. Any decent-looking tree that can survive browsing by deer and can handle that meadow's unimproved heavy clay, sodden much of the time, is welcome there. Apart from those maybe-hawthorns, the youngest trees inherited from the previous owners are probably twelve years old. I bought a Russian olive and a Franklin tree this summer for the upper lawn. I must buy some other new trees, so that there will be another cohort to follow the twelve-year-olds.

Even imperfect trees are worth the trouble. Trees are awesome examples of life rooted to one spot. Each one has inherited a uniquely evolved strategy for occupying as large a volume as it can of the open air available in its neighborhood for the chlorophyll in its leaves to grab light and make the energy necessary for flowering, fruiting, seeding, and reproducing. While its trunk widens annually, its boughs, branches, and twigs spread an ever more intricate web in the air. If the tree is deciduous, that web is starkly visible in gray and brown throughout the winter, becomes obscured behind a light green mist of buds in spring, then vanishes behind the more solid dark green covering of leaves during the summer. Then, in the next winter, it doesn't vanish entirely, as most perennials do around here, but stays right there in gray and brown silhouette again — until one morning after the first overnight snowfall we wake to see it suddenly transformed into an exquisite negative image of itself.

And those transformations are nothing compared to what happens when the trees flower in spring and lose chlorophyll from their leaves in the fall. Debbie Nevins told us we need more interesting trees, and I agree. I would like more clouds of pink and white in the spring and summer, more bright colors or berries in the fall. What trees could deliver? Looking through catalogues and books I can see some candidates. There are some tough, very common trees that are said to grow easily in our soil and in zone 5 that should provide the additional color we would like. A saucer magnolia, with big waxy pinkish-purple flowers in spring: that was one of the pencil-thin trees that failed me, but I'm up for trying again. Ann loves magnolias. We have a wonderful mature shadblow at the edge of our east woods, with a cloud of delicate white flowers in spring, so it would be good to have a young one coming along to take its place when it dies. A Japanese tree lilac, more substantial than the shrub lilacs, would have large white flowers in late spring. Then there are cherries: a Higan cherry would have white to pinkish flowers in spring, and a Yoshino cherry would bring a little bit of Washington's Tidal Basin to Chatham. And, talking of Washington, if those little things in the meadow aren't hawthorns, a tough, prickly Washington hawthorn with white flowers in late spring and red fruit in the fall would be excellent there. Then, for some summer color, a devil's walking stick (*Aralia spinosa*) would have white flowers, but I would have to be careful: it can be very invasive. A panicled goldenraintree has yellow flowers in summer, and Ann likes yellow. In the fall, the leaves of a black tupelo could turn yellow, scarlet, orange, or maroon.

I would especially like to see more displays of the sort that our two big old crab apples put on in spring: dark pink on the corner of the house and bright pink by the swimming pool. Those particular trees are disease-prone and don't flower reliably every year, but when they flower well, they are the stars of the place. In my opinion, no massing of simultaneously flowering perennials — or annuals, for that matter (not that we have any) — could remotely compare to their spectacular display, and our place could definitely accommodate more of them without overkill. I would plant them at the edges of the lawn. Seeing all that color blazing from individual trees, I couldn't resist walking Ann over to look closely: hundreds of thousands of flowers on each tree. We would be dazzled. And bees would be humming all around us.

 CHAPTER 21

Open and Closed

THE OPENNESS OF GINGER which Ann and I love we might not even like if it were open to the public, so to speak: that is, if the hundred and seventy-five yards at the bottom of the lower lawn were not screened from the street by trees and shrubs. I wonder whether we would have even considered buying it if we hadn't felt a sense of enclosure when we drove in to see it for the first time. Openness within enclosure is what we like, the luxurious combination of spaciousness and privacy. When I cleared some shrubs five years ago that had been obscuring the trunks of a big cedar, a big white pine, and a big oak at the entrance, Ann was very unhappy. She saw that she could now be seen from the road as she walked from house to swimming pool, and she didn't want to have to make sure she was wearing something every time she did so. It took three years for shrubs in a slightly different position to grow tall enough to substitute for those I had cleared. Now we have our screen again and also a good view of the big trees, but during those three years the gap in the greenery was a constant irritant.

Walling or fencing or hedging in a garden hasn't generally been considered neighborly by Americans, as Michael Pollan shows in his wonderful *Second Nature*. Most Americans have preferred, and still prefer, to show off their gardening to passersby, not hide it away. However, there are practical reasons for erecting a fence, as Michael Pollan found out. It can protect plants from big animals. Hence my dreams of a high fence around our nine and a half acres to keep out Doreen. Then, too, marking boundaries is important for a sense of ownership, and blocking out the outside world is important for a sense of relaxed private pleasure, no less important than curtaining or shuttering the windows of a house on the road. Visible boundaries are surely built into the very idea of a garden, defining it literally and figuratively.

I wouldn't, for instance, call the acres around Jack Millard's house, where a line of peonies in the lawn inspired me to try out a thin crescent of irises in our upper lawn, a garden. What I see there I like very much: the line of peonies parallel to the road; a shrub border set back parallel to the line of peonies, with lawn between them; and a long mixed perennial border perpendicular to them on their right. The choice of plants and their arrangement are pleasing, as are hundreds of thousands of plots around houses in the suburbs and towns and villages all across America, but they are all arrangements of plants in a semipublic space. They may be gardened by gardeners, but they aren't gardens.

Maybe this is the ex-Brit in me coming out. In the congested British Isles and Europe, spaces around houses have, doubtless out of necessity, been enclosed by walls, fences, and hedges for a long time. And the British especially have made the most of those enclosed spaces, filling them with pleasing arrangements of annuals and perennials to make what I consider real gardens. In the best ones, the boundaries act like frames around works of art. You feel you have closed a psychological door behind you as you enter them, leaving the mundane public world behind. We felt a little of that when we first drove into Ginger, and it's what I want other people to feel when they arrive.

Not that I want to go so far as to create what must be the most extreme example of an enclosed garden, namely, a walled garden, a rectangle enclosed by high brick walls with solid wooden doors or iron gates. I couldn't afford it, we don't have the flat land it needs, and anyway it may represent something of old-time England and Europe that I came to America to get away from. Walled gardens are highly artificial creations, and very formal. Nothing could be more different from them than the informality, the seeming randomness of design, dictated by the terrain of Ginger. And yet I recognize that a walled garden is a realization of a sort of ideal I respect. Its walls emphasize the specialness of a particular place, a place devoted only to gardening. It's an inner sanctum. If I had flat land, and lots of money, I might be tempted.

One walled garden that I realize has meant a lot to me over the last twenty years doesn't exist, at least physically. It's the one in Frances Hodgson Burnett's great children's book *The Secret Garden*. Ann and I hadn't read it until we read it aloud at bedtime to Emily and Lucy. I think Ann started reading it to them and I took over, because I could handle Dickon's broad Yorkshire accent easily. The religious-magic element I found sentimental and embarrassing to read out loud — I hadn't read it myself ahead of time, so I had to make quick decisions about what to skip as I read it to Emily — but that comes toward the end of the book, by which time I had got thoroughly caught up in the story. I was happy to read it again to Lucy two years later, and that time I knew what to skip. Some of the books I read to our daughters last thing at night put me to sleep as I was reading them aloud, but not this one.

There is plenty of drama in the story. Mary, orphaned in India, is sent to live in her uncle Archibald Craven's big house on the Yorkshire moors. He has a misshapen back, is still mourning the death of his wife (Mary's mother's sister) ten years before, and is absent for months at a time. Mary, skinny and thoroughly spoiled, discovers her bedridden cousin Colin only when she hears him crying in another part of the house. Colin is even more spoiled than Mary, and he is apparently crippled like his father. The plot revolves around how these two somewhat obnoxious young characters can ever become spiritually and physically healthy and whether they will ever experience a loving relationship with Colin's father. Dickon, the uneducated country boy with the Yorkshire accent and a way with plants and animals, plays a pivotal role in Mary's and Colin's redemption.

The children are so vividly portrayed, and they are each so important in the story, that the book could well have been titled *Mary* or *Colin* or *Dickon*. Or it could have been titled *Mistlethwaite Manor*, after the huge and gloomy house. But Burnett's brilliant stroke was to make the other place in the book, an abandoned garden in the grounds, the means of regeneration and redemption and to make it secret. The very idea of a secret garden immediately raises questions: why is it secret, and what's it like? Burnett knew that no young character, faced with such a secret, could resist trying to penetrate it, and that no young reader could resist a well-told story with "secret" in its title.

A tragedy in the garden before the events in the story accounts for its secrecy and for the state of affairs in the house at the beginning of the story. The garden quickly becomes the focus of the story, and what happens in the garden accounts for the happy ending. Surely never since Eden in Genesis has a garden played such an important role in the fate of a story's major characters.

Among all the many reasons why Burnett's story appealed to me, even though I was a middle-aged male living in America nearly a century later than its events, there was this one: it was about an orphaned child sent to live in the Yorkshire moor country, as Faith and Roger and I had been. And most readers, I imagine, can identify with a child's excitement at finding a secret place, penetrating it, keeping it secret, and then sharing it. The secret place in Michael Pollan's early life was the little place between a hedge and a fence in the backyard of his parent's quarter-acre suburban plot. "Whenever I needed to be out of range of adult radar, I'd crawl beneath the forsythia's arches, squeeze between two lilac bushes, and find myself safe and alone in my own green room." In my case it was a spot on the Yorkshire moors, a small hollow with bracken and heather for walls and with grass grazed smooth by sheep.

Emily and Lucy used to go off and play in a hollow in a slate quarry in the woods at Fred. Pine needles covered the slabs of slate enough to make the ground and sides soft. They were within earshot but we couldn't see them, so they had the place to themselves for however long they wanted to be out there. They took an old coffeepot and some mugs and plates and played at making meals. One spring we found that over the winter the coffeepot and mugs and plates had been used as targets by hunters. The coffeepot was riddled with holes and the mugs and plates were in pieces.

Where would a child at Ginger go off to get away from parents for a while? Probably somewhere in the woods surrounding the lawn, perhaps in one of the parts I haven't cleared. There's one place nearer than that, though, that might attract a child. It's an area of tangled weeds and trees behind the big compost heap at the back of the garage. I squeezed a few yards into it six years ago as part of my getting-to-know-the-place exploration, and I found a room-sized rectangular space bounded by a few feet of broken-down concrete block wall. It had been abandoned, and now briars, honeysuckle, sumac, a couple of white pines, an oak, and vines were growing inside and all round it. It would be an eyesore if I cleared the area and a big job to get rid of the concrete, so I am happy to leave it hidden there. But a child might be delighted to find those walls and might be tempted to make something of the space inside them.

Frances Hodgson Burnett doesn't give the dimensions of the secret garden, and I have always thought of it as not very large, although much larger than the size of a room. Perhaps forty feet by eighty: would that be about right? That wouldn't overwhelm a little girl. It would be large enough for her to run around in but small enough for its plants to be close and friendly and small enough for her to think of it as hers. But I haven't seen one that size. We saw some walled gardens in England one spring, and they were big. The one at Castle Howard in Yorkshire, for instance, conveniently halfway on our drive from Acaster Malbis to Hutton-le-Hole, is an amazing eleven acres, large enough to make the walls look small in the distance when you stand in the center. I tend to think of our nine and a half acres at Ginger as large, but I am comparing it to the gardens I remember at Hutton-le-Hole and elsewhere in England or to gardens on one-acre plots in England and America, whereas our whole property could fit easily into Castle Howard's walled garden, which itself is just one small part of the whole huge estate.

But come to think of it, there is an area of our property whose dimensions are not so far from what I had imagined Mary's garden to be and which could become an excellent garden, fifty feet by sixty. It won't ever be secret. It's very conspicuous, right in the middle of the property, but it's already the place on the property that kids head for. Why haven't I been thinking of this as "garden"? It's the exception at Ginger. The property slopes, but this is flat. The property is informal and looks natural, without a straight line anywhere except for the path through the meadow, but this area is highly artificial and rectangular. The property is open, but this has a wooden fence around it. The fence encloses the swimming pool, a wooden deck, and on one side two trees and five red-twigged dogwoods and on the other two small tree pits without trees.

The wooden decking has deteriorated so badly that it is potentially dangerous. We had decided to replace it with a new wooden deck until we saw recently a couple of swimming pools with a thin strip of bluestone around them, and lawn around the bluestone, and we realized that this could look much better than wooden decking without (perhaps) costing more. We could also have perennial beds in this enclosed area, where at last we could grow some plants that Doreen likes but might be deterred by the fence from reaching.

Ann monitors the pool's chemical status and skims its surface every morning. (I vacuum it, pour chlorine into it, and haul out drowned rodents.) You can't skim quickly, and Ann finds the few minutes of slow, quiet movement calming, and she loves to see the results of her work: clear water with a sparkling surface. I can imagine the whole experience would be even more pleasurable if she were surrounded by some lawn and a colorful border, or several borders, of flowering perennials. We might even try to keep that patch of lawn weed-and-wildflower-free and make the borders strictly rectangular, with crisp edges parallel to those of the swimming pool and the fences. It would be the one formal garden in the place, an enclosed garden within an open landscape which is itself enclosed.

I like the idea. One of my favorite parts of Central Park is the Conservatory Garden, the only formal garden — actually three gardens in one, six acres — enclosed by iron fencing within the generally informal and natural-seeming 843 acres of the park. Much of it is very open, with expansive views across huge lawns, but it is itself a rigid rectangle enclosed by walls but further enclosed by the "walls" of the city's tall buildings.

Each of the three Conservatory gardens is very beautiful in its own way: the north one French, the central one Italian, and the south one English. The whole is a real *garden* garden, where we can see flowering perennials, clipped shrubs, and fine trees in superbly harmonized arrangements. I like the English garden particularly. At its center there is Bessie Potter Vonnoh's 1926 sculpture of Dickon and Mary from *The Secret Garden*. Our friend Sara Cedar Miller includes two beautiful photographs of this sculpture in her *Central Park, An American Masterpiece*. One of these photographs shows the green sculpture from behind. It stands in a lily pond, surrounded by the muted colors of varied perennials and a backdrop of taller trees. Mary's body is the central feature of the photograph. As Dickon plays his flute, a bird alights in the bowl Mary holds in her fingertips. The whole sculpture — bronze figures, bronze bowl full of water, and bronze bird in the bowl — is a birdbath.

In the other photograph, the birdbath is in use. We see Mary and Dickon from the front. Sara has caught long drops of water falling from the birdbath. All is green, the sculpture and the surrounding plants all green, except for the light on the water and one blob of muted red on the breast of an actual robin. Dickon is looking ahead as he plays his flute, Mary is looking down as she carries her bowl, the bronze bird is looking to the right as it takes a bath in the bowl, and the real robin is on the edge of the bowl looking up, probably swallowing the water it has just sipped from the birdbath as Sara snapped the picture.

REWARDS

CHAPTER 22

Why Do It?

I IMAGINE MOST gardeners aren't often asked why they garden, and I imagine most gardeners don't ask themselves that question. They just garden. Or they just love growing vegetables or flowers, or creating a good-looking place outdoors — what more to say about it? That's been my attitude, too, on the whole, until recently when I got sick, blamed the gardening I had been doing, and found myself asking myself why I do it. Five years ago I spent the morning of July Fourth having a gash in my hand sewn up in the hospital. Two winters ago I spent six months with back pain from a herniated disk, and last year I contracted Lyme disease, whose symptoms were fever, listlessness, and weakness, lack of appetite, and a backache so painful that I couldn't sleep for a week. The culprit in each case was gardening, or the way I garden, which may be more recklessly than I should. When I'm cutting down white pine boughs, I know where they are going to fall, but that July Fourth I hadn't calculated how a particularly big one — which must have been the hundredth I had sawed in a few days — might bounce back up at an angle off the ground. (I'm lucky it was only my hand it gashed.) I know how not to pick up heavy stones and how not to dig, lift, and throw clods of heavy clay, but I bet it was building a low stone wall or digging a new perennial bed last fall that herniated my disk. I tuck my trousers into my socks before I work in our meadow or our woods, I spray my clothing with DEET and I examine myself carefully when I take a shower later, but a tick got me anyway, in the middle of the back. And it was three weeks of Lyme, especially that week of nonstop back pain and no sleep, which finally made me wonder: is it worth it?

Ann saw what that tick did to me, and she swore that if she stepped outside the house again she was going no farther than our decks. She didn't put me on the spot by asking why on earth I still wanted to garden, she merely suggested that if I continued to garden the way I had been, I should wear a space suit. No, it was I who wondered out loud whether I should give it up, or do it somewhere safer, or pay someone else to do it for me. A week of misery seems a lot longer than that when you are in the middle of it.

It made me ask myself what it would be like not to garden. I have had almost as many injuries from playing tennis, something I am as passionate about as gardening, and I can just about imagine not playing it, especially as cable TV serves us fans pretty well and promises to serve us even better in the future. But not gardening? The prospect is so bleak that it has made me ask myself the follow-up question: why is gardening what I want to do more than anything else? What on earth has made me so obsessed? Why is a day spent digging, hauling, raking, clipping, spraying, mulching, composting, planting, transplanting, watering — all that exhausting repetitive work — exactly what I want to be doing?

It's not all hard work all the time. I do take time, plenty of it, to just wander and sit and look and think. But the physical side of gardening is no small part of its appeal. Gardening is as physical as you want to make it. You can work up a sweat and make your muscles sore very easily with all the bending, lifting, pushing, and pulling. You can get fit and stay fit. And you have something more to show for it than the conditioned body which you can get with weights and a treadmill at a gym. Exercise in the garden is so good not because of the exercise but because of the gardening, so the question still stands. What's so special about it?

There are so many things I like about this occupation — preoccupation — that I find it hard to know where to start. But one place to start is with the feeling I get when I drive up our driveway at Ginger after being away, anywhere, for only a few days, turn off the ignition, open the car door, and step out to look around. It's somewhat how I feel every time I walk from Manhattan's streets into Central Park, especially when I penetrate the Ramble there, or when I leave Brooklyn's streets and make for the center of the Brooklyn Botanical Garden. Our garden is in only one way comparable to those places (there's far more lawn and trees than flowering plants), but I get the same feeling in it as I do in them, a special sense of calm and relief: yes, this is a very good place to be. Then, because we own it, I get a sense too of immediate interest: how is it different from when we were here last? What's new in the perennial beds? Other people may step out of the car and simply want to go straight into the house and fix a drink, but Ann is usually weeding the nearest perennial bed before I have taken our cases from the trunk, and my feeling as I look around, before even approaching the trunk, is pure pleasure.

The overall impression would strike most other people too as pleasant, I think, but when I look at individual perennial beds, I see all sorts of things I want to fix. Should I replace all those hostas Doreen has been chewing on with plants that Doreen doesn't like? What would thrive and look good there? Maybe I can improve that sedum's chances of having an easy life by relieving it of some of its pushy gooseneck loosestrife neighbors. But then, where to put the gooseneck loosestrife? I like the constant figuring and refiguring.

I would give up so much if I didn't garden. I like watching the processes: annuals growing from little shoots into mature plants which flower in a great burst of color and keep flowering and flowering until finally frost gets them; perennial shoots swelling and reaching upward and outward until they too flower at last, then they seem to die, but no, they reappear the following spring to go through the whole performance again. New life in spring year after year: every year new excitement. I like yearning for spring during those awful last weeks of winter. Well, it's a bittersweet pleasure, having to wait and wait when I don't want to wait a day longer, but knowing that any day now the air will feel warmer and the first shoots will be poking up from the soil, and — how could I do without that feeling?

Maybe I could, but I don't like the thought. My list of reasons goes on and on. I like looking at a perfect individual flower, and smelling it. I want to congratulate it. I think of it as an achievement, the plant's and mine. I'm a card-carrying believer in the Pathetic Fallacy, ascribing human thoughts and feelings to nonhuman things. I mean, I know they don't have them, but so what? I can't help yelling at a rose that has scratched me as if it had been waiting for just this moment to get me. Which certainly goes for ticks and the deer that carry them. But I'm a sucker for beauty: I love human beauty, like everyone else, but consider that perfect flowers are some of the greatest examples of beauty you can find anywhere on the planet in your lifetime, so I can't help thinking of plants that produce them as friends I'm lucky to have.

At the same time, I like what the very impersonal sciences have to tell me about plants. I like learning about the relationships of plants, one to another; about their classification into family, genus, and species; about the evolution of their forms; about the shapes of plants from root tip to stem tip, the shapes of their underground parts, the arrangements of branches on a stem, leaves on branches, flowers on stems, petals on flowers, reproductive parts within the petals; about their strategies for reproduction involving wind, birds, or insects; how their specialized methods of luring birds and insects so often lure us too. I like knowing that there is so much to learn that I can never stop learning.

Books, catalogues, and magazines are a large part of my gardening pleasure, and you can't get ticks from them. Then there are other people's gardens. I like comparing the good ones, which are all unique, to other gardens I have seen in person or in print and to our own. I like reading about their plants, and about what other plants can be grown successfully in our area of the country. Then I also like reading about gardens in other areas of the country and of the world. But reading isn't as good as reading and gardening.

I wonder whether all gardeners share these feelings.

I don't know. I can't recall anyone's saying why he or she likes to garden. The subject hasn't come up. Maybe it is only beginners who are asked why are they are getting into it, not people who have been doing it for some time, who may tend to think or say, "Isn't it obvious? I just love it." There may also be plenty of people who don't care one way or another about the plot of dirt and lawn that came with their house: they feel they should keep it neat, and that's it. For me, the feeling that I am making something, or changing something, in my garden is an addiction. I like hearing Ann report on what she has seen in our garden. "That view up to the entrance to the woods is really great," for instance, when it took a long time to see that it might be good, a long time to make it look good, and plenty of time to make the changes seem invisible. And when she sees details: "Did you see that white flower near the ferns and pachysandra?" It's a bloodroot, and the flower lasts only a day or two, but she saw it in time. I like hearing other people exclaiming at the things that amaze me too.

In the context of our search for wisdom as we live with other humans, observing how they deal with living and dying, the knowledge and experience derived from gardening may be small potatoes. But thinking about how we can live our lives better can surely be even more rewarding when we consider our lives in the context of all those other lives around us. You don't need acres. Several square yards of garden is a microcosm of nonhuman life.

We are lucky enough to have woods and a meadow, lawn, slopes, flat parts, and a number of separate perennial beds, with different plants in each. Ginger is a lab for observation and a theater for very slow but orchestrated performance, and I like not only hoping that I can make it look better than it does but also knowing that as soon as I leave it alone it will become something different. Well, that too is a bittersweet pleasure, knowing that nature can and will carry on very well indeed (although differently) without my help. Plants will have no problems taking over from humans, if humans die out, unless of course we mess things up so badly that we take them down with us.

I find the slow pace of gardening particularly attractive. Worms and ants move fast compared to plants, but together they constitute a very slow-moving picture. Gardens change so slowly over the course of a year and over many years that one day (even all twenty-four hours of it) is a snapshot to be compared to distant days. You see worms moving, leaves swaying, but you can't see the garden changing. So you are always remembering what it was like not this morning but last week or last month, and you are anticipating what it will be like next month and next year. I like constantly making those comparisons.

The mind is very good at forgetting bad things. The further in time I get from my three weeks of Lyme-induced misery, the easier it will be to forget them. But right now I fear that I am going to look at particular parts of our property as particularly dangerous, and even the whole place with different eyes. I used to look out from our windows with nothing but excitement and delight. Now when I look out I am anxious that I will see something moving out there, a big animal with a white tail, gray-brown coat, and maybe antlers. Of course, whether there are deer or not, the scene is beautiful. The early morning sunlight on the weeping willows, the network of spiders' webs glistening with the dew on the lawn, and all the changes during the day until that soft evening light grows dark again — day after day, those pleasures will be weighing against the memory and dread of danger.

I was ending my third week of antibiotics when I walked out onto the lawn, knelt to photograph the straight green path through the brown meadow, walked up to the top of the slope in the east woods where I saw that one of the white cast-iron chairs had broken, knelt again to fix it, and walked back inside with the chair. That evening I found another tick on my leg. It was mid-November and I couldn't even walk around, maybe kneeling a couple of times, without covering myself with repellant? I was beginning to convince myself that of course all the pleasures of gardening throughout the year outweighed the pain of those three weeks, but suddenly I wasn't so sure again.

I looked again at the double-size postcard of a 1963 painting of a stag I had bought at the Museum of Modern Art's retrospective of Gerhard Richter's work in 2002. It's the antithesis of Sir Edward Landseer's dramatic 1824 painting *The Monarch of the Glen,* the only other painting of a deer I can think of. Richter's painting is mostly thin black outlines of skinny tree trunks and leafless branches on pale gray — maybe a winter scene. That's what had appealed to me: the dense tangle like the one I had had to clear in our west woods. The stag in the middle of the picture is more realistically painted than the trees and so can't help being beautiful, but it's blurred as if it was photographed walking, and a strange diagonal shape, presumably a tree trunk near the viewer, divides the picture into a left half and a right half and also blots out the middle of the animal. In my present state of mind, I wanted the animal to keep walking out of the picture, leaving that pleasant patterning of trunks and branches and taking its damn ticks with it.

There are two dead willow trees lying in the long weeds at the border of our west woods. I should chain-saw them, but if ever there was a place sure to be full of deer ticks waiting for a warm-blooded animal to come along, that's it. I'll postpone the job. Let time tell me what to do. Next spring I'll probably want to be out there doing everything I've been doing for the last five years, but with greater caution. Meanwhile, though, this gardener is worrying, wondering, waiting, and reading.

CHAPTER 23

Where to Find Inspiration

ACCORDING TO RECENT Harris polls, gardening has been for a number of years among the seven most popular leisure activities for Americans (with reading, watching TV, spending time with family and/or kids, fishing, going to movies, and computer-related activities), which I take to be excellent news for the people involved, for the plants involved, for the land involved, and for the country. If asked what I believe in, one of the first things I would say is that gardening can be good for the soul (whatever that is). I know it's good for mine. Walking on lawn instead of concrete, digging in soil, watching a plant grow and flower, it's very good for — almost necessary for — my spirit.

And there's another dimension. I think of Mark, whom I met in the spring of our first year on our property. We were having our perennial beds prepared for the spring by Callander's (protective netting taken down, rose canes pruned, edges crisply dug, mulch and fertilizer applied). It was a pleasant warm day, and Mark, the foreman of the crew, was sweating, filthy, and bleeding from scratches on his arms, a state I became very familiar with in subsequent years. While we were chatting, Mark said that one of the things he liked about his job was that he was making art. I don't remember the verb (making? involved in? creating?), but I do remember the noun, art. Here he was in a garden that was nothing to look at, certainly nothing to photograph unless conceivably as a "before" picture to compare to an "after" picture in a few months' or years' time; he would be doing the same sort of heavy labor all day long the next day, and the next day — day after day through the growing season — in other people's gardens; and he called it art. It was inspiring.

As it happens, I haven't heard anyone mention "art" in connection with gardening since then. And I don't expect to. In fact, I bet that most gardeners would look over their shoulder to see who is standing behind them if they were accused of being artists. Nevertheless, that's what many of them are, and many gardens are unquestionably masterpieces of fine art.

In gardening books, I do occasionally come across the word. I'm not referring to books devoted to garden design, where I would expect to see the word used (although, come to think of it, I don't remember its popping up in the very few I have consulted). And I'm not thinking of all the indispensable books whose indexes I consult when I am wondering about a particular plant or problem. I'm thinking of the books that were written to be read rather than consulted (consulted, too, but primarily to be read and reread), books with a narrative or argument or both, books that pack so much wisdom about plants and planting into their pages that when their authors do step back and generalize about their art or their overall aims or what inspired them, I sit up and pay special attention. I'm like Joseph Epstein, who in his essay "But I Generalize" (collected in *The Middle of My Tether*) says, "I am afraid I am one of those people who continues to read in the hope of sometime discovering in a book a single — and singular — piece of wisdom so penetrating, so soul stirring, so utterly applicable to my own life as to make all the bad books I have read seem well worth the countless hours spent on them." I couldn't agree more. I read for wisdom, but also, when I read gardening books, for inspiration.

Occasionally I find it in passages in which the gardener-author reveals how he himself or she herself is inspired. In some of these passages the word "art" comes up, and I notice that when it does, the gardener-author often makes a connection between the aesthetics of gardening, the health of plants (on which everything else is based), and his or her own spiritual health, and I am prompted to think yes, that connection is what it's all about. When a garden looks good, I feel good in it.

I have recently been preoccupied with seeing what I can do with the groundcover garden on the slope of our east woods. The bottom of the slope receives several hours of afternoon sun, but the top, which has been cleared of undergrowth and low branches, nevertheless remains in shade all day long. It's both a question of which plants will thrive best in which sections of the slope and also an aesthetic question of how to effect a natural transition between lawn and woodland. When I turn to a classic on this subject, Gertrude Jekyll's first book, *Wood and Garden* (1899), I come immediately, in her Introduction, to one of those stirring passages. It starts quietly:

> I am strongly for treating garden and wooded ground in a pictorial way, mainly with large effects, and in the

second place with lesser beautiful incidents, and for so arranging plants and trees and grassy spaces that they look happy and at home, and make no parade of conscious effort.

(I can't say that I have managed to follow this advice. I am asking for what I do on the slope to be looked at as a picture, but I have defined the particular area to be looked at with a large semicircle of stones, so the conscious effort is pretty obvious.) But then her paragraph rises to a paean:

> I try for beauty and harmony everywhere, and especially for harmony of colour. A garden so treated gives the delightful feeling of repose, and refreshment, and purest enjoyment of beauty, that seems to my understanding to be the best fulfillment of its purpose; while to the diligent worker its happiness is like the offering of a constant hymn of praise. For I hold that the best purpose of a garden is to give delight and to give refreshment of mind, to soothe, to refine, and to lift up the heart in a spirit of praise and thankfulness.

I read that and agree a hundred percent. But then I think, would I describe what I am doing when I garden in those terms? How on earth can the slope I am working on live up to that?

Jekyll, who started as a painter, created gardens and wrote books about gardening, both of which were an inspiration to generations of gardeners. Roughly half a century later, Russell Page also started as a painter, also created some of the great gardens of the world, and also inspired generations of gardeners. He wrote only one book, but if there were one gardening book I would take to a desert island, it would be his *Education of a Gardener*

(1962). Debbie Nevins, who completed one of Page's gardens (illustrated in Mick Hales's *Gardens Around the World: 365 Days*), says she read Page's book three times when she was starting out. Page, like Jekyll, strove for a visual effect: "Whether I am making a landscape or a garden or arranging a window box," he writes, "I first address the problem as an artist composing a picture." And like Jekyll, he strove for a "theme of peace and unity which, as I see it, must be a main aim for any garden if it is to be considered as a work of art."

Russell Page never created a garden for himself. However, he ended his excellent book with an extraordinary climactic chapter, "My Garden," which is a daydream of how he would, if he could, design his own garden. This vision, precisely described, of his ideal garden is a paean of praise and thanks. One paragraph sums up so much about planning a garden as mental labor and artistic aspiration that I have to keep rereading it. It starts off with a self-conscious statement of aims that echo the very language of Jekyll:

> A garden really lives only insofar as it is an expression of faith, the embodiment of a hope and a song of praise. These are high-sounding words but wherever I set my aim, high or low, the achievement, by the very nature of things as they are, is bound to fall far short of them and a too modest aim may well result in an insignificant achievement.

This speaks to my problem. I am trying to make my garden on the slope look good, but what Page is telling me is that that is not enough. My aim should be to make it look so good that people will feel good looking at it. But how? How to switch on the light bulb? Then I remember that the inventor of the light bulb said that genius (which Page had) is one percent inspiration and ninety-nine percent perspiration. Hard work — there is no substitute for it.

Page's first aim, he continues, is "to leave a place more beautiful than he finds it," but that's not enough. He must please not only himself but others, so another aim must be to understand the point of view of other people. But that's not enough either. He must also understand all the processes that go to make a garden, "the rhythms of all humans as well as all vegetable processes."

> I draw and draw, searching for a composition which will come right in its own time only, perhaps at once, perhaps after hours and days of work. Of course the answer is inherent in the problem, and I find the solution only as soon and as clearly as I see all or enough of the factors which compose the problem. So now my aim includes my own necessity for clearer thinking. You see now to where this leads, for a finer quality of thinking comes only with a wiser heart and where must I look to find the heart's wisdom?

This sublime paragraph ends with Page's reminding himself of all these aims as he wrestles with putting his ideas on paper, making calculations and lists, all the time thinking of the mundane "vagaries of behaviour of plants and men, soil and weather." It's a self-portrait of a humble human looking for, laboring for, inspiration as he sets the loftiest goals for himself before even picking up a spade. And as I read and reread that paragraph, and think about the ajuga and pachysandra and vinca and aegopodium and lamium and ferns I am hoping will fill out and control the weeds on that slope, and about all the other projects I have started and half-finished at Ginger, and about the fact that I haven't once planned with paper, pencil, or word processor, I can't help feeling very small, a beginner. I've hardly started.

Which is when I need to reach for Henry Mitchell, who was a humble gardener but a very unhumble writer of funny, democratic, and very on-target columns for the *Washington Post* in the last quarter of the twentieth century. In "How Does Your Garden Grow? Any Way You Choose," in *Henry Mitchell on Gardening* (1998), Mitchell offers encouragement to people like me:

> Gardeners are not quite so different from one another as you might think at first. Even Versailles [which Mitchell can't stand] has some attractive plants in it, and even a jumble of marigolds, petunias, cleomes, chicory, tomatoes, and onions presided over by a fig tree against a shack — even in such a garden there is often a degree of self-conscious attention paid to the aesthetics of the arrangement.
>
> As long as there are plants at all, and as long as the gardener is human, and as long as the garden is an important part of the gardener's leisure, there will be a bond or a spirit between all gardens of whatever type.

That makes me feel better. Mitchell is so earthbound and sensible. But there are times when he too rises to a higher level of discourse. In "Up and Down the Garden Path — Or, Designs for Gardening" in his collection *The Essential Earthman* (1981), he describes gardening as an art form and a spiritual quest:

> Gardening is not some sort of game by which one proves his superiority over others, nor is it a market-place for the display of elegant things that others can-

not afford. It is, on the contrary, a growing work of creation, endless in its changing elements. It is not a monument or an achievement, but a sort of traveling, a kind of pilgrimage you might say, often a bit grubby and sweaty though true pilgrims don't mind that. A garden is not a picture, but a language, which is of course the major art of life.

These passages are rare in the advice-filled, plant-and-soil-directed pages of Jekyll and Page and Mitchell, almost as rare as the sort of comment Mark made in our garden is in whatever conversations about gardening I have taken part in every week since then. But they have the same effect, coming from people whose chosen job it was, as his was, to work tirelessly on their craft, sweating and getting dirty to create something beautiful. They inspire.

And what inspired Mitchell? In "The Beauty of Natural Selection," in the first collection, Mitchell writes in December, not the most inspiring of months, how beautiful common holly and common ivy are at this time of year, and hopes he never loses his admiration for these very "ordinary plants." Then he looks around his bedroom:

> By my bed is a sorry little collection of half-dead plants (which will be fine once they can go outdoors again at the end of April) that give me the greatest pleasure but that remind me how ignorant we are about the deep mysteries of life.

And he looks around his garden:

> When I peer about my little garden, which is sometimes so beautiful, I never admire this plant or that without a certain awe that beneath the surface and

structural beauty that even the coarsest human eye can see lies a creative dynamic truth at the heart of all life that is still hidden from simple men like me but that will one day be clear to all.

He's thinking of how science, following Darwin's footsteps, will one day enlighten us, but his language could be taken for religious, as could Jekyll's and Page's. These three great gardeners, in their choice of language in these passages (plants looking happy and at home — delightful feeling of repose and refreshment — purest enjoyment of beauty — theme of peace and unity — expression of faith — embodiment of hope — song of praise — kind of pilgrimage — creative dynamic truth at the heart of all life) reveal a shared bond and spirit. Aren't we all, they are asking, if we have chosen to work with plants, however ordinary, each in our own way searching for Paradise?

 CHAPTER 24

Roger's Wood

THE LAST TIME ROGER visited us, we cut down several dead trees in the west woods, and Roger chain-sawed two of the largest curved boughs in such a way that when we propped them four feet apart, dug their thick ends into the ground, and leaned their thin ends together, they made an arch eight feet high. We positioned it in an open area about ten yards below the circle where Em and Dave got married. As long as it lasts, it's our equivalent of the stone arch "folly" in the wood at Acaster Manor.

There are some other whimsical presences in our west woods. I cut down most of our dead trees at the base, but about fifteen I cut down at heights of three to six feet and put rocks on the stumps that were left standing. The results are phallic in some cases (can't help their looking like that), humanoid in others. There's one near the rock with the bench on it which I was able to cut at about twelve feet because the rock rises steeply behind it and I could reach it from there. The stone on that one looks somewhat like a shtreimel, the wide Jewish fur hat.

Roger has some presences of his own in his fifty-acre self-contained tract of woodland called Stub Wood. His presences are sculptures or, rather, a sculpture of ten figures positioned together. Roger commissioned the work, which consists of ten simple pieces of wood sawed from the trunks of three evergreens that had been growing in Stub Wood. Each piece, between six and ten feet high, has two holes drilled near the top, like eyes. The group is called *The Guardians.* Roger contributed the evergreens, the sculptor produced a maquette (which Ann and I saw when we visited Roger and Jenny), Roger executed the sculpture according to the sculptor's directions after we left and positioned it in Stub Wood in a place and manner subject to the sculptor's approval. Roger's very excited about it. We'll see it there the next time we go.

We visited Roger and Jenny toward the end of April, early in a month-long tour of England and Scotland visiting family and friends. Acaster was halfway on the trip north. Then a week later we stopped off again at Acaster on our way south. We always walk around Stub Wood when we are there, so last spring we walked around it twice, and I'm very glad we did. The Manor garden, across the road from Roger's house, is worth walking around, and it gives me a pang whenever I do, but it isn't what it was when Roger and I were children, let alone what it was earlier in the twentieth century, and Roger isn't responsible for it now. The farm and Stub Wood, on the other hand, which our father rented out to a local farmer when we were small, have been Roger's since he bought Faith's and my shares in the property in the late 1960s, and he has improved both beyond recognition. If I want to find inspiration for what I am doing in Ginger's woods, I need look no further than to what my brother has done with his Acaster wood.

From his house it's a long walk on a straight raised road across the flat five-hundred-acre farm to the wood, or it's a short bicycle ride, which is the way Ann and I usually do it, or it's a drive, which is the way we usually do it with Roger. He drives us there very slowly so we can take in the views. On the left we look across large, flat, hedgeless fields all the way to the invisible river Ouse and to trees and a few buildings on its far bank; on the right we look across similar fields to a fence parallel to our road in the distance. Roger tells us what crops we are passing — rape, barley, sugar beet, oats, potatoes. He points to the birds — partridges, plovers, lapwings — that have risen at the approach of the car. Then we enter Stub Wood.

I think I vaguely remember walking up to Stub Wood's border with our parents during World War II, but if we did, we couldn't walk in it. The British Air Ministry, which owned the airfield next to the wood, had taken it over and had built bomb shelters (that is, shelters for bombs) throughout the wood and hardtop roads to reach them. It must have shocked our parents. Fire had swept through the wood in the 1920s, and it must have seemed to them that what was being done to it now was just as damaging, only this time the damage was permanent.

Roger bought the wood back from the air ministry when he took over the farm himself, and he quickly realized that what might have ruined the wood forever had instead preserved it forever. The bomb shelters could be demolished and their rubble taken away, but removing all the roads would be too big a job, so he could never clear the wood and its roads to farm it. On the other hand, he saw too that the wood was beautiful:

it was a haven for wildlife, and the roads were the perfect way to walk, bicycle, or drive through to look at it. He would enjoy making it something of a special haven at the end of his farm and an asset to the community, a place many other people would want to walk around besides the family.

Stub Wood is second growth, like our woods at Ginger and like much of the once-farmed and now tree-covered northeastern United States. But Stub Wood is "ancient replanted woodland," having remained unfarmed for over three hundred years, and that's how it will remain. Roger set about improving it — he calls it "managing" the wood, but it's much more than that. It used to be a chaotic tangle of young trees, bracken, briars, and rhododendrons. The rhododendrons I do remember when I was a teenager. They were so big that you could walk into them and feel you were in sizable rooms. They were a fine sight when they were in bloom, but they had become aggressive weeds, and their dense evergreen foliage kept all competition out of fifteen acres and made them impenetrable. Roger cleared them from all but four acres.

This last spring the rhododendrons at Acaster weren't in flower, but halfway to Hutton-le-Hole, where we drove with Roger and Jenny to see Hammer and Hand House and the moors and the daffodils at Farndale nearby, we stopped off at Castle Howard. It has, among many mind-boggling features on its property, one of the greatest collections of rhododendrons in the country. Over eight hundred species and varieties of rhododendron have been planted in Ray Wood, and April and May are the months in which they flower. Ann and I felt like kids looking at candies in a shop window. Rhododendrons are the plants our deer like best, so apart from two shrubs, which we stake and net in winter, we have ruled them out at Ginger.

Roger dug trenches throughout Stub Wood to drain it, and in one section he planted thirty-five hundred young oaks, beeches, and birches. The first time we saw them, ten years ago, they were a dense grid of vertical white plastic pipes with a skinny stem and a few leaves poking out of the top of each. By last spring the plastic had gone and what we saw were trees branching and leafing out. We also saw many not-so-young ornamental trees which Roger had planted to enhance vistas.

We stopped the car and got out to look around. There were acre-size pools of white among the trees, an amazing sight. Wood anemones were in flower. They are extremely difficult to establish, so their growth in profusion is a rare sight, a hallmark of ancient woodlands. For most of the year, you don't see them even there: they are just rhizomes in the soil. But in February they start sending up deeply lobed leaves and, in April, delicate white flowers. I love our three-foot-tall cultivated 'Honorine Jobert' anemones at Ginger, but these little things down on the ground are individually just as beautiful and en masse breathtaking. As we drove farther into Stub Wood, there were more acres of them. They were everywhere.

Roger showed us where the land suddenly subsided. A tentacle of one of the world's largest coal mines ran directly under the farm at this point. The mine had ceased production in 2003, after extracting 121 million tons of coal in ten years from over 260 faces in the Vale of York, accessed by 460 miles of underground roadway — enough, the press release said at its closing, to build a tunnel from York to Paris. The mining company had signed agreements with landowners that subsidence, which they tracked by satellite, would be no more than a stated number of inches. Subsidence exceeded that number considerably on Roger's farm, putting his prime fields (those on the left as we drove to the wood) at risk of flooding when the Ouse ran high, and sure enough, in the spring of 2000, the worst flood in four hundred years occurred, costing Roger several major crops. The mining company compensated him for his loss and created a flood barrier by raising the road to Stub Wood several feet.

The wood was buzzing with bird activity, and we saw hares and a few deer bounding away, which got Roger excited. Deer aren't yet his enemy, as they are ours, but I can't imagine it will be long before he too wants them out of there. He was delighted ten or fifteen years ago when he discovered badgers in the woods. He encouraged them by building a home for them, complete with pipes and wire mesh — a big job requiring heavy equipment. The badgers ignored the place for several years, but then moved in. Roger and his children watched them at night and photographed them. Now he is not so delighted. The badgers have proliferated, moved from the artificial home to a number of different homes, some of them in the middle of his fields, creating a big problem for the machines he uses to fertilize and harvest the fields. He showed us one of their homes in the side of a ditch at the edge of a field, a huge area with paths worn shiny and flat by their scurrying feet.

But the threats to Stub Wood have been more serious than badgers in recent years. The first threat, in the 1980s and 1990s, was when a developer planned to spend two hundred million pounds to build a new town on the neighboring airfield. Roger led a protest group against this development over several years and eventually prevailed. The airfield has now been designated part of York's "green belt," protected from development.

The second threat was in the spring of 2003, when the seclusion and beauty of Stub Wood attracted, of all people, ravers. On three separate weekends, about fifty teenagers from cities all over the north of England, some even from London, converged on the wood for weekends of food, drink, and loud music. Roger and his neighbors were alarmed at the noise in the middle of a Friday night. Roger went to investigate and the ravers were pleasant then, telling him how wonderful it was to get out of the city and be in such beautiful surroundings, but their vehicles had gouged ruts in the ground, and Roger had to clear up bonfire and food garbage. By Saturday they were tired and were running out of food and drink and drugs, and by Sunday morning they were threatening. In England you can't be prosecuted for trespassing unless you can be proved to have damaged the property you have invaded, which is difficult. Roger's padlocks were no deterrent, so he had to block the entrances to the woods with bigger obstacles.

Although the wood is private property, he makes sure that it can be reached by a large number of enthusiastic local walkers, birdwatchers, wildflower lovers, and naturalists, who are just as interested as Roger in preserving the beauty of this natural environment. On our first visit last spring, Roger let them know that the wood anemones were in flower and that the bluebells should be out the following week. It's a special time of the year for these people, some of whom come regularly in organized groups.

As for us, our month in England and Scotland took us to some of the most beautiful parts of each country: the Cotswolds, the Peak District, the North Yorkshire

Moors, the Yorkshire Dales, the Highlands, the Low-
lands, the Lake District, the Suffolk coast, the South
coast. We planned one visit to a famous garden and
made unplanned visits to several others. We then spent
a week in Umbria, where we also visited some gardens.
But among all those sights, which for a gardener were
different visions of perfection, none was more memorable than Roger's Stub Wood in full flower.

I find ungardened acres of color more inspiring than
farmed or gardened acres. Roger's acres of rape, for instance, are a brilliant display of excellent farming, but as
acres to be contemplated, their yellow is too bright and
solid (and their smell too unpleasant, but that's a different story) to compare with his acres of tiny white wood
anemones. The most wonderful acres of yellow I have
ever seen anywhere were the pale yellow drifts of daffodils which Roger and I used to visit every year in Farndale, when we lived three miles away at Hutton-le-Hole,
and which Roger and Jenny and Ann and I saw fading
on our trip last spring.

In Umbria, what from a distance seemed to be
stretches of red plastic fencing turned out, when we
came near, to be great drifts of poppies in field after field
of grass. That wild red in a field is the exception to my
earlier generalization that a little bright red is enough.
What is true for gardens isn't true for ungardened nature. If red flowers are growing naturally in the wild,
nestled in green foliage, you can't have enough of them.

And that's true too of blue. Maybe it's true of any
color when it is muted by surrounding greenery, but it's
especially true of blue. How often do you get to see acres
and acres of blue in a wood? Stub Wood has them every
spring, and Roger and Jenny said that last spring was an
exceptionally good year for them. We could hardly be-

lieve it when we came back to Stub Wood that second time. We got out of the car and waded among them. We couldn't stop exclaiming at what we were seeing. They were everywhere, on and on. I think our woods are pleasant to walk in, but they haven't gone one square yard beyond brown and green. Roger's wood has forty acres of bluebells.

LIFE AFTER DEATH

CHAPTER 25

Weeping Willow

UNTIL LAST SUMMER, a weeping willow grew at the very center of our property. When visitors saw it for the first time, they probably assumed that it was the reason the property had been called Willow Hill. It was the huge tree visitors saw ahead of them at the end of the driveway as they drove in, and if it had been raining, they could drive through the stems hanging from its boughs and feel they were going through the flapping felt towels of an automated car wash. When they stepped out of their car, it towered above them and billowed around them. It was the one tree on the property that was likely to lodge in their memory. Which is where now it has to remain. Its physical presence at the end of the driveway is a thing of the past.

I have cut down a lot of big trees at Ginger without thinking much about it: they were dead or dying, and I knew that the crowded area they were occupying would look better, and that their neighbors would find life easier, without them. But this was different. This tree was not only not dead, it was the best-looking tree on the place. When Ann and I told friends we were thinking of cutting it down, their reaction was an incredulous "What? Oh no! Why on earth would you want to do that?"

We asked them in turn whether they had ever seen a tree leaning at such an angle over their parked car. This in itself wouldn't have been sufficient evidence against the tree, considering, for instance, that the superb weeping willow Thomas Pakenham photographed for his *Meetings with Remarkable Trees* leans over the people snacking at tables and chairs in London's Hyde Park at roughly the same angle as ours leaned over our friends' cars. But I bet that tree hadn't been hollowed out by ants, as ours had. When we suggested to our friends that they peer through a gaping hole in the tree's trunk to see its empty core, they could see we had a problem, and when we told them that a huge bough falling from the top of the tree last year missed Emily, her husband, Dave, and me by minutes, they agreed that, yes, we should probably do something about it. Our friend and neighbor Ruth, who despite her name knows when it pays to be ruthless in the garden, said, "You know, you're going to be very pleased when you've done it."

But the decision was painful. Most trees are anonymous, living out their sometimes long lives unnoticed among other trees, but when a tree has been allowed to stand for decades on its own with plenty of space all around it, spreading wide as it keeps growing up and up, there's a good chance that it will at the very least catch the attention of most humans, perhaps even striking awe into any who come close and look up at it. And if it's a weeping willow, it has the added attraction of that unmistakable shape. Those cascades of limp stems — gray-brown in winter, bright yellow in early spring, then pale green when the buds become leaves, all swaying together in the wind — add up to a unique combination of massive size and feathery softness. And if the tree is in a special place on your property, as ours was, it will almost certainly occupy a special place in your affections, as ours did.

It was the place that was the problem with our tree, as it often is with weeping willows. Fred Callander, the Chatham nurseryman and landscape designer, said, "Everyone should have a weeping willow, but never near anything important." They look splendid and grow conveniently fast, but underground their roots are strong enough to penetrate drains, while aboveground their branches are annoyingly weak, shedding parts of themselves all year long. Our tree was in the ideal place to be admired from a distance, but in a dangerous place if you got close to it. And it was the one place where people were guaranteed to collect before and after coming into our house. We had to kill the tree before it killed one of us.

It was far too big a job for me and my chain saw, so we contacted an arborist, who came with his crew and with cherry picker, chipper, truck, several chain saws, and ropes. He maneuvered his little box high among the branches, roping them, cutting them, and lowering them to his crew below, who fed them into the chipper. Within minutes the tree which had delighted us and previous owners — for how long? forty, fifty, sixty years? — was a jagged skeleton. In a few minutes more, there was only a stump.

Most trees are as anonymous in death as in life, although they may be just as useful to humans after death as they were when they cleaned and moistened the air with their transpiration. Around me here, as I sit at my desk, the decks and deck railings are from trees, the siding on the outside walls and the shakes on the roof are all from trees. The joists and studs throughout the house are from trees, as are the floors in all the rooms except the kitchen, the walls in three of the rooms, and the ceilings in most of the rooms. All of our bookshelves, our tables, our desks, many of our chairs, the paper in our books and magazines and in my printer are all from cut-up and processed trees. I wonder where and when they lived, the trees from which all these materials are derived, and I wonder what they looked like when they were living.

I do know the provenance of the logs in our fireplace. Before I cut them, they had been sections of the trunks of ironwood and maple trees on part of the east slope of our property, which I cleared to make the woodland garden of groundcovers. And I do know where the weeping willow is now. For a couple of weeks after it had been cut up and taken away it was a huge pile of chips and leaves just inside the entrance to our property. It sat there heating up, fermenting and steaming, and smelling like nothing so much as tobacco. I haven't smoked tobacco for decades, but I loved being near this heap. Mushrooms appeared on its top. Over the course of several days I moved the pile, load by load, to cover the two paths up the slope on either side of the ground-cover garden. The willow has become two curving carpets, which feel soft to walk on and will remain very visible on the slope as long as I keep them weeded.

The stump, near where we park our car, will stay there until we decide what to do with it. It has a huge hole in its middle, from which I dug four wheelbarrow-loads of dark brown spongy dust for our compost heap. Above and around the stump there's a whole lot of openness, which Ann and I find refreshing. Ruth was right. Now we have an unobstructed view of the line of fourteen large weeping willows between our meadow and the woods to the west. It was they, not the central weeping willow, which gave their name to the property. Ants may be getting at them too, but they are in what Fred Callander would consider the right place: at a distance, where we can admire them without anxiety.

CHAPTER 26

Elm

THE BIGGEST LIVING THING on our property is an elm at the edge of our upper lawn in the east woods. It's very impressive when you stand directly under it and look at how far up and out it reaches, although it isn't as conspicuous from a distance as it would be if it were growing in the middle of our upper or lower lawn. But there's another elm that is just as big and isn't in the lawn and is conspicuous. It's at the edge of the upper lawn in the west woods, directly opposite the living elm, and it's conspicuous because it's dead.

When we bought Ginger, the elm in the west woods was living and blended in with all the other trees around it, but it had fewer leaves on it each year until finally they were all gone. Long bark strips fell away from the two trunks rising from its base, and little branch ends fell down, so now its almost white trunks stand out against all the neighboring trunks and its top bare branches are silhouettes above the fully leaved trees around it.

The tree is at the top entrance to the west woods (which has three entrances: this top one, the one Roger and I worked on in the middle, and one at the bottom end of the straight path through the meadow), and it serves to signal the entrance like a huge pillar. Two years ago a bough came crashing down onto the upper lawn at the entrance into the woods — just where I might have been walking — and broke in two. One end speared the lawn so deeply that pulling it out was as much work as chain-sawing and carrying off all the chunks. The top of the tree is now asymmetrical, and from one point of view, the whole thing is ugly. And it could conceivably be considered dangerous. I can imagine an arborist looking at it and saying, "Take that one down." But I'm the only one who goes into the west woods at that point, so the likelihood of the tree's falling on anyone is, in my opinion, as good as nil. And I like it, ugly dead branches and all.

The tree has an important advantage over all the other trees on our property. Birds congregate in its bare branches, and they can be seen easily there, whereas in all the other fully leaved trees they can't. And in winter, when the deciduous trees have lost their leaves and birds have a large choice of bare branches to sit on, they appear to like it more than its neighbors, maybe because it's such a high perch.

The top branches of the dead elm are totally visible from our bedroom, the dining room, and the kitchen. If the crows that wake us in the morning aren't stalking across the upper lawn, they are silhouetted in the branches of the dead elm. And quite often some drama appears to be going on up there, as if alarms about some enemy are being broadcast as loudly and energetically as possible. Little birds like the tree too. Sometimes there are ten or twenty of them, and they can get very animated, especially when a hawk decides to sit with them for a time. Once, four or five bluejays (not so little, I suppose) forced a young hawk off its perch up there and chased it to the corner of our roof, then to the railing of our front deck, then to the central weeping willow, then back to the dead elm in a repeated cycle for half the morning until finally the hawk took off.

Pileated woodpeckers like our property, and we like them, despite what they do to our living trees. Watching their cartoon-like antics as they dig to get at ants in the tree trunks, spraying three-inch-long chunks of light-colored wood all around them, is sheer entertainment, especially when two of them are working together, as we saw through binoculars late last winter.

In early June I was walking up there when I saw what looked like a long beak in one of the two big holes at the back of one of the trunks of the dead elm, and sure enough, as I stood there, the beak was withdrawn. Pile-ateds were nesting there. I brought the camera with me and waited patiently until I saw two small heads with long beaks and bright red crowns. Roger commented, when I e-mailed my photograph of them, that they looked like prehistoric animals. For a week there was a lot of pileated noise in that tree, then silence. The young ones had flown.

Whenever there's a big storm I look anxiously up at the dead elm to see if it is standing, and if so, how many branches are left. It may be years before the big tree finally succumbs to gravity, but I'm not looking forward to seeing it gone. It's not just that we hope to see the pileated woodpeckers returning year after year to their hollowed-out home, which I suppose may be hoping for too much. It's that such a fine stage for woodpeckers and crows and bluejays and hawks and countless other small winged bodies will have vanished. After death that tree has hosted the most visible vital aerial activity on the property. We would have to wait until the other big elm, the one at the edge of the east woods, died and offered its bare branches as a new performance space. I wouldn't be surprised if whatever killed the elm in the west woods doesn't get to that one soon, but I don't want to hasten its end. I'll be content to hear the birds among its leaves and imagine what's going on up there.

CHAPTER 27

Gardens Change

DESCRIPTIONS OF GARDENS can't keep up with their subjects. Gardens give the appearance of being static because, after all, plants don't move; but plants get moved, and they move anyway, with or without our help. They go through the processes of living and growing and dying, and they are moved by the weather. Gardens don't seem static when you see them after having not seen them for a few weeks or months or years, and they don't seem so static when big things happen suddenly, as was the case in our garden when that big dead elm fell down in a storm. Suddenly an important visual element of our garden — not just the network of ever-bare branches but the constant bird activity in them — was gone.

It was there as usual when I looked up at it first thing in the morning to see the crows I could hear screaching in it. It looked to be rock solid, its two trunks standing steady while all the trees around it were bending wildly in the wind, but when I looked again after breakfast, all I saw there was one trunk with its top snapped off just above the pileated woodpeckers' home and a three-foot jagged stump at the bottom of where the other trunk had been. I suppose it was precisely the fact that it had dried out and was brittle and couldn't bend in the wind that doomed it. I walked up to see the huge trunk stretched in a broken line on the ground with its top branches now smashed in a cluster at the end. I was glad that it fell inward into the west woods instead of out onto the upper lawn, where moving it would have been an urgent job, but I'm sad that it's gone. For a long time Ann and I will be looking up there automatically to see birds, and all we'll see is a space in the tree line. The birds have lost their high perch with good visibility all around, and we have lost our easy view of them.

You can't describe a garden as it is because it isn't — any longer. It was. And now? It's becoming — as always. Describing a garden is describing change. Luckily, perhaps, the processes of life and death and the forces of nature change gardens so slowly that most changes are at any one moment almost imperceptible, as when buds swell to become leaves and leaves change color. Our eyes don't see the changes happening, and we're tempted to think at times, perhaps in the spring, perhaps again in midsummer, and perhaps again in late summer, "This is it. This is what we've been waiting for. This is the garden." But every time we say it, two days of growth change everything: whiskers of new leaves blur edges, weeds appear from nowhere. And then every so often the change is dramatic, as when our elm was flattened in seconds by a storm, leaving me with a big clean-up job, not to mention an unwanted pond at the bottom of our lower lawn, and all the other parts of the lawn so sodden that footprints show where we have squelched across them. A week of wind and sun is needed to dry them out, and meanwhile I can't take the golf cart, or even the wheelbarrow, over them. Every week, every day, in the garden brings changes.

Gardening is dealing with change. And gardening is changing a garden, most obviously when we are improving it — as I hope I am doing when I move plants around or when I slice a crescent of irises into the middle of our upper lawn — but it's changing a garden even when, for instance, we are working hard seemingly *not* to change it, that is, when we are satisfied with the way it looks and are trying to keep it looking like that. Mowing the lawn here is changing millions of grass plants. Pruning is changing hundreds of twigs and branches. Every maintenance job — digging, watering, edging — is changing today's status quo.

All the gardens around us are changing all the time. One evening four years ago a storm hit Ruth and Leon's garden during dinner, and the next morning their view down to the stream had been changed. The swollen stream had swept whole trees away. Another year they cut down a huge central willow, letting sunlight reach the plants below. And last year they planted six river birches where the one big willow had been. When trees, the biggest and most permanent features of a garden, change, they change its structure. But the details of the picture — the shrubs, the perennials, the ground covers — fill in the picture, and a catalogue of all the changes Leon and Ruth have made to their garden's details week after week over twenty years would be exhaustingly long.

Each time we visit Roger and Jenny at Acaster, we see a changed garden behind their house: new fencing one year, an arch another, new plants being tried out, annual and perennial beds in different shapes. Stub Wood has new ornamental trees, new vistas opened up. The

Acaster Manor garden has over the years lost many of the features which I loved as a child, although the resulting unobstructed view from the house across the lawn to the lake has its own beauty. If that garden, or the gardens which my aunts made at Hutton and which now have new owners, were to look the same now as they did when I knew them decades ago, I would feel I had entered a disturbing dream.

Even classics of the gardener's art, preserved seemingly for the ages in the color pages of a book, must change. During our visit to England last spring, Ann and I saw the garden at Barnsley House, which turned out to be somewhat different from the one I knew from the glorious pictures in Rosemary Verey's account of its creation in *Making of a Garden*. It was raining on the day of our visit, and the brightest color (almost the only color) among all the greens, was the pale blue of thousands of forget-me-nots. Even more different, though, were the eight yews lining the main walk from the front of the house, which in the book are nine-foot trees shaped like vases swelling out from the bottom to about five feet wide, narrowing, then swelling out again at the flat top. Last May those yews were a very different shape: they had been reduced to three-foot-tall, four-foot-wide bowls with gently rounded tops, as if filled with a foaming liquid.

Gardening is working with nature and also against nature, encouraging some plants to grow and others not to grow, exposing some plants to the weather, protecting others against it, nurturing growth and controlling it, changing a place and dealing with its changes. Hugh Johnson, who gave his *Principles of Gardening* a subtitle perhaps designed to encourage beginners like me, *The Practice of the Gardener's Art,* describes the difficulties facing the would-be artist working with a living, ever-changing medium in the first paragraphs of his Preface:

> A poet is limited to the dictionary, a sculptor starts with a block of stone, but a gardener starts with a plot that is frozen one day and flooded the next, here in sun and there in shadow, teased by wind and tantalized by drought, plagued by insects, toyed with by birds, mined by moles. No two gardens are the same. No two days are the same in one garden. And yet on this flapping canvas an amateur, often without previous experience, and holding the instruction book in one hand, tries to daub a vision of a better world — or if that is flying a bit high, at least to grow vegetables and feed the family.

I don't grow vegetables, so I would say that if I'm not trying to daub my vision of a better world on Ginger's flapping canvas, I'm trying at least to make visitors like what they see enough to be happy to come back — my unwritten mission statement.

Not that I mind thinking of what I do as grappling with an art form. But it certainly is a very odd art form. Not only can you never accurately describe a garden, you can never finish one. A garden simply keeps going, changing a little, changing a lot, never staying put. A photograph of a garden shows it as it looked from only one position at only one point in time. A lot of photographs in a book such as Rosemary Verey's show only some views of it before the book was published. What about all the other views? And hasn't the garden changed since then? (Yes, it has; we saw that.) Showing a garden to visitors a select number of days in a year is about the best that can be done, conveniently ignoring all the preparation before those days and the cleanup and letdown after them, not to mention the years before and after. What could do justice to a garden's changing over time? An impossibly slow, long movie might go some way toward capturing a little of the reality of a garden's changing and being changed — between two points in time — which no one would want to see. In literature, books such as Joseph Eck and Wayne Winter-owd's *A Year at North Hill,* which take readers through the cycle of changes in a garden in a year, perhaps do it best.

In art, Monet saw areas of his beloved garden at Giverny change in the changing light of the same day or the changing light of different weather in different days, and returned again and again with literal canvases to record his impressions. He created masterpieces that, even when verging on abstraction, describe beautifully how his Japanese footbridge, his garden path, and his water lily pond could change before his eyes. It became an obsession in his old age, and I for one wish he had had even more time in his life to indulge it in yet more paintings of his chosen subjects. That's what a garden is: the same place, different every time you look at it.

Giverny deteriorated after Monet died, but it was resurrected by generous donors and gardeners dedicated to showing what had inspired his late masterpieces. But perhaps they were doing more than that. Weren't the scenes Monet created with trees, shrubs, perennials, annuals, water, and a wooden bridge as great as his depictions of them? Wasn't he as great a gardener as he was a painter? Wasn't his garden, changing as all gardens do, a masterpiece of the twentieth century?

Which brings to mind Central Park, which Sara Cedar Miller calls in the subtitle of her book *An American Masterpiece*. She said that when her proposal for a book on the park was declined by twenty or so publishers, she asked herself, "Why on earth don't these publishers want to publish a book about the most important nineteenth-century American work of art?" Then she had a revelation: she hadn't described the park in quite those words in her proposal. She immediately revised it to explain the park as a work of art, whereupon Abrams, arguably the best art book publisher in the country, agreed to publish the book and the Henry Luce Foundation agreed to support the Central Park Conservancy's portion of the book's cost. In the book, she states her opinion in the first sentence of her Introduction — "Central Park is the most important work of American art of the nineteenth century" — as a fact.

Is that provocative? Frederick Law Olmsted, the designer of the park with Calvert Vaux, considered himself as much an artist as any sculptor, painter, or architect, and he described the park as a work of art. But a century and a half later, we are still not used to having gardens, parks, or public spaces described as works of art. Maybe it's because, although there are histories of gardens and landscape design, there isn't a thriving criticism of them, as there is of art and architecture, literature, music, and the movies, a criticism that measures gardens or parks against one another by carefully considered criteria. When did you read a bad review of a garden?

At any rate, Sara Cedar Miller's first sentence startled me briefly, and then I thought, yes, of course! What could conceivably compare? In fact, I wonder whether Central Park may not be the greatest American work of art — period. Some great buildings, or some built environments, or some other parks may come close. Olmsted himself considered Prospect Park, in Brooklyn, better than Central Park. And of course some great books and great movies speak to the problems of individual, social, and national relationships and aspirations more directly and more powerfully. But just think of the millions of people who are still being awed and refreshed every year by those 843 acres in the middle of New York City, deliberately designed in the mid-nineteenth century to look natural and beautiful for their benefit. I'm with Sara Cedar Miller: Central Park gets my vote.

And yet Central Park, which seems such a secure haven, such a known quantity, so reliably itself while the buildings change around it and the traffic courses through its sunken cross-streets, is itself a living, changing thing. It is a different place for different people and for different occasions: trysting place, open-air theater, birdwatcher's destination, concert venue, zoo, skating rink, carousel, woods, baseball diamond, boating lake, jogging and bicycling track, site of Christo's and Jeanne-Claude's *Gates*, botanical exhibit, peaceful retreat. Some of the park's glorious architecture remains as it was built in the 1870s, but even some of its buildings have vanished or been added. And as for the huge lawns, lakes, woods — they have all changed shape. The Conservatory Garden didn't exist until 1937. And although some features of the planned plantings haven't changed since they were designed, the plants themselves have. The Mall, for instance, the only straight line in the park, is the magnificent promenade the designers envisaged, but the elms that were planted on either side of it in 1858 died that year. Their replacements were dying by the end of the century; the ones we see were planted around 1920.

Those elms lining the Mall constitute, together with the elms along Fifth Avenue, one of the largest stands of elms in America, so many around the country having been decimated by Dutch elm disease. It's sobering to learn how carefully they must be monitored to detect or prevent this disease which, once it is established, can kill such big trees so quickly. There are several photographs of them in Sara Cedar Miller's book: three recent ones in different seasons, and once when they were small. Looking at the photograph of the small elms, we can glimpse what a disaster it would be if they died off.

Our own dead elm, now lying in the west woods, probably won't lie there for long. I'll chain-saw it into logs. If for some reason I decide to leave the tree lying there, it will imperceptibly change as it rots and disintegrates over the years, adding nutrients to the ground beneath it as it disappears. Or, taking the long view, new owners of the property may see other uses for its wood, as they may for much else around here. They may fill in the swimming pool and grass it over, as we did the broken-down concrete block swimming pool at Fred when we bought it. They may drain our lawns and start vegetable gardens in them, plow up the meadow and seed a crop there, build flights of steps in the upper lawn, chop down acres of the west woods, lay down new driveways or plant new trees, pursuing new visions.

Or maybe new owners will like this place the way it is. Meanwhile, the tallest tree here, and one of the most beautiful, is still the elm at the top of our east woods. I have recently been taking down dying and weedy trees in front of it to give us an unobscured view of it. At present it appears to have a full quota of leaves, but who knows how long it will last? When it dies, it will be the place with the best sightlines for birds and the place where we will get to see them most easily from our kitchen and bedroom. Then it too will dry out and crash down in a storm. Maybe I shouldn't wait for that to happen but buy some proven disease-resistant varieties of elm and plant them now for future generations. I must add that to my annual list of jobs for this year.